# history at source

# IRELAND and ENGLAND

## 1798-1922

Joe Finn and Michael Lynch

Hodder & Stoughton

A MEMBER OF THE HODDER HEADLINE GROUP

# ACKNOWLEDGEMENTS

**Author's acknowledgement**
To the memory of Joe Finn, whose idea this book was and who had drafted a substantial part of it before his untimely death.

The publishers wish to thank the following for permission to reproduce illustrations in this volume: Cover - National Library of Ireland. The Trustees of Cambridge University Library, pp. 42 (top), 52, 62 (bottom); The Illustrated London News Picture Library, pp. 46, 47 (top and bottom); Hulton-Deutsch, p. 54 (bottom); Punch Publications, pp. 43 (top), 48, 55, 56 and 60; Imperial War Museum, p. 62 (top); The British Library, pp. 43 (bottom), 45, 49 (top), 53 (bottom), 57; Public Record Office of Northern Ireland, pp. 42 (bottom), 61 (top); National Library of Ireland, pp. 44, 51, 54 (top), 58, 61 (bottom); National Museum of Ireland, pp. 49 (bottom), 63 (top); Trustees of the Ulster Museum Belfast, p. 59 (bottom).

The publishers also wish to thank the following for their permission to reproduce material in this volume: The Bodley Head for the extract from *Landlord or Tenant: a View of Irish History,* Magnus Magnusson (1978); Lawrence & Wishart Ltd for the extract from *Ireland Her Own: an Outline History of the Irish Struggle,* T.A. Jackson (1971); the extract from *Paddy and Mr Punch: Connections in Irish and English History,* R.F. Foster (Allen Lane, The Penguin Press, 1993) © RF Foster, 1993, reproduced by permission of Penguin Books Ltd; Weidenfeld & Nicolson for the extracts from *The Green Flag: A History of Irish Nationalism,* Robert Kee (1972); the extract from *States of Ireland,* © Conor Cruise O'Brien 1972; Methuen & Co. for the map from An Atlas of Irish History, Ruth Dudley Edwards.
Every effort has been made to trace and acknowledge ownership of copyright. The publishers will be glad to make suitable arrangements with any copyright holders whom it has not been possible to contact.

**British Library Cataloguing in Publication Data**
Finn, Joe
Ireland and England: 1798-1922. - (History
at Source Series)
I. Title II. Lynch, Michael III. Series
941.508

ISBN  0 340 575085

First published 1995
Impression number   10  9  8  7  6  5  4  3  2  1
Year                1998   1997   1996   1995

Copyright © 1995 Michael Lynch

Typeset by Sempringham publishing, Bedford
Printed in Great Britain for Hodder and Stoughton Educational, a division of Hodder Headline Plc, 338 Euston Road, London NW1 3BH by Page Bros (Norwich) Ltd.

# CONTENTS

# APPROACHING SOURCE-BASED QUESTIONS

This book aims to provide a set of key documents illustrating Anglo-Irish relations between 1798 and 1922, and to suggest how the material can be best analysed and interpreted. Questions based on documents form a compulsory part of all A level history exam papers. Some boards include documentary questions in outline courses and all make them a dominant feature of depth studies. It is not unusual for as much as 50 per cent of the total marks to be allocated to the document section. The questions vary; some require the study of prescribed texts, extracts from which appear on the exam paper for analysis. Others do not indicate specific texts but set detailed questions on documentary extracts that might not have been seen previously, but which candidates should be able to analyse by reference to their knowledge of the course.

Some questions test the candidate's ability to read and understand a historical document. Others examine background knowledge of wider themes or probe understanding of special topics. The most demanding are those which ask for evaluation of a historical document.

All papers indicate the marks on offer. These are a guide to the relative importance of the question and the proportion of time to be spent on it. As a rule of thumb, each mark offered should correspond to a point of fact or analysis. This should not be followed slavishly however; candidates can waste valuable time trying to find an extra point merely to satisfy an apparent numerical requirement.

Care should be taken to deal with the question as set. Examinees asked to evaluate a document will gain little from paraphrasing it or giving irrelevant details about its background. As well as showing understanding of sources, candidates at this level are expected to have an appreciation of historiography; that is, to know something about the problems in writing history. Being able to spot bias, attitude and motive in the writer of an extract is important. Questions requiring comment on the `tone' or the `colour' of a passage are common; and in responding to such questions, candidates should ask themselves: Does the writer seem angry, bitter, confident, detached, involved? Is the document an official report or a personal reminiscence? Does it suggest that it was written for a particular audience or is it a general statement? Is it propaganda or objective reporting? If candidates train themselves to do this, they will develop analytical skills that merit high marks.

# INTRODUCTION

The story of Ireland's relations with England is not a happy one. From the time of the Plantagenet conquest of Ireland in the 12th century, to the creation of the Irish Free State in 1922, the native Irish regarded themselves as being subject to the rule of a series of uncaring English governments. By 1798, the time at which this book opens, distinct differences in culture, language, social structure, and religion divided England and Ireland. These were later given a particularly perceptive definition by Benjamin Disraeli. In 1844, he described the condition of Ireland in these terms:

**A dense population in extreme distress inhabits an island where there is an Established Church which is not their Church, and a territorial aristocracy the richest of whom live in distant capitals. Thus you have a starving population, an absentee aristocracy, and an alien Church, and in addition the weakest executive in the world. That is the Irish question.**

Sixteenth-century England had undergone a religious reformation. Thereafter, its Protestantism was an essential expression of its character as a nation state. Ireland, however, had remained Roman Catholic. Equally for the Irish, therefore, their religion became part of their identity as a people. This major difference of faith deepened the mutual Anglo-Irish antagonism that had developed over four centuries.

English governments from the time of Elizabeth I onwards had strength-ened their hold on Ireland by dispossessing the native Irish from their land and giving it to loyal Protestants from England and Scotland, most of whom settled in Ulster. This policy was made easier to enforce by the 'flight of the earls' in 1607, a strange incident in which 90 of the Irish chiefs abandoned Ireland for the Continent, leaving Ulster leaderless. Yet even without their traditional leaders, the native Irish so hated the plantation policy that they rose in rebellion in 1641. This rising was a violent outburst of pent-up frustration that was finally crushed only by the severest brutality. During the period of the English Republic (1649-60) Oliver Cromwell undertook a savage suppression of Irish resistance, which culminated in an even fiercer application of the plantation policy. By the late 1650s some 80 per cent of Irish Catholics had been deprived of their land.

The remaining Catholic landowners supported the deposed Catholic monarch, James II, in 1689 in his Irish-based campaign to recover his throne. His defeat by William of Orange in 1690, left the rebellious landowners in disarray. This increased the domination of the Anglican property-owning class, whose supremacy was reinforced by the highly restrictive penal laws that were imposed on Catholic landowners, effectively depriving them of the rights of citizenship.

To these political and religious restrictions were added heavy economic burdens. Arguably, the heaviest of these resulted from the practice of absentee-landlordism. The plantation policy had created a situation in which the majority of estates were owned by Englishmen who seldom lived in Ireland and who regarded their property primarily as a means for raising capital to spend elsewhere. Wealth was not reinvested in the Irish economy. The poverty and insecurity of tenants was such that even in good years they were barely able to feed their family and pay their rent. In bad years they could do neither and faced eviction. By the end of the 18th century the bulk of the Irish people led precarious lives on the verge of landless destitution.

The French Revolution, which began in 1789, coincided with a particularly turbulent period in Irish history. The radical ideas of the American Revolution had already been eagerly taken up by Irish intellectuals. Events in France were greeted with similar enthusiasm, and in 1791 the Society of United Irishmen (SUI) was formed. Taking as its inspiration the French revolutionary ideals of liberty, equality, and fraternity, the SUI went beyond merely reformist ideas and sought a democratic republic on the model of the recently-founded USA.

Events took a new turn when England went to war with France in 1793. Fearful that the French might try to play upon Ireland's revolutionary sympathies, the English government offered the Irish Catholics a limited measure of electoral enfranchisement. Not only did this concession fail to win support among the Catholics, it aroused the anger of the Protestants of Ulster, and led to the forming of the Orange Order, dedicated to the maintenance of Protestant supremacy. When the long-expected Irish rebellion came in 1798, the Orangemen helped to crush the Catholic rising, thus intensifying sectarian bitterness. Although some Protestants were to be found in the ranks of the rebels, as in the rising in Wexford, the overwhelming body of Protestants sought to protect their privileged position by appealing for direct rule to be imposed from Westminster. Pitt's government was keen to oblige. The French Revolution had deepened economic depression and increased agrarian violence in Ireland. Desperate to retain its grip on Ireland, the English government pushed through the Act of Union, which ended the separate Irish Parliament and formally made Ireland part of Great Britain [Chapter 1].

The government then reneged on its promise that union would be accompanied by the granting of emancipation – the extension to the Catholic population of full civil rights. The Irish Catholics felt betrayed. As a consequence, post-union Anglo-Irish politics were dominated by the emancipation issue. Daniel O'Connell, a radical Irish politician, established himself as leader of the emancipation campaign. In 1829 he led his Catholic Association to a remarkable victory when Wellington's Tory government, fearing civil war in Ireland, reluctantly introduced the Catholic Relief Act, which granted all the main points in the emancipation demand [Chapter 2].

Having achieved emancipation, O'Connell went on in the 1830s to build an Irish party of MPs at Westminster who pressed for the disestablishment of the Anglican Church in Ireland. Encouraged by a number of Whig reforms in the 1830s that weakened the grip of the Anglican Church, O'Connell began a campaign for the repeal of the Act of Union itself. However, Catholic emancipation had transformed Irish politics. The customary supremacy of the Protestants now seemed threatened and they began to organise in defence of the Union. This frustrated O'Connell's efforts and a group of younger men emerged from the repeal movement, who styled themselves 'Young Ireland'; they rejected O'Connell's constitutional methods and advocated violence as the only means of breaking the English hold [Chapter 3].

The 1840s were dominated by the Great Famine. The three consecutive potato harvests of the years, 1845-7, were destroyed by disease. The effect was to decimate the Irish population that had doubled during the preceding century [Chapter 4]. The bitterness of the famine years was deepened by the perceived failure of the English government to take steps to relieve the misery. Young Ireland adopted a policy aimed at the forcible expulsion of the English. Planned outrages occurred widely and the Westminster Parliament responded with twelve coercion acts between 1847 and 1857. These merely provoked further violence and led to the founding of the Fenian movement in 1859. The Fenians asserted that Ireland was independent but temporarily in bondage to England. Claiming to be the true authority of Ireland, they organised a series of bombings in mainland Britain during the 1860s [Chapter 6].

The first Liberal ministry of W.E.Gladstone (1868-74) began with the declaration that his mission was to pacify Ireland. A number of measures were introduced dealing with Ireland's religious, educational and land grievances. However, these reforms failed to stem the rising tide of evictions and the violent reactions that invariably followed. By the time Gladstone returned as Prime Minister in 1880, Irish agitation had taken a significant new course with the emergence of the second great Irish leader of the century, Charles Stewart Parnell.

An Irish protestant landowner with a strong anti-English background, Parnell believed that once Ireland was given back its own Parliament, it could solve its own problems. A skilled parliamentarian, Parnell organised obstructive tactics by the Irish Nationalist MPs to wring concessions from the government. In 1885, when the Nationalists won almost every Irish seat and held the balance of power between the Liberals and Conservatives in the Commons, he helped convince Gladstone that the only way to achieve Irish 'contentment' was by granting Home Rule. This Gladstone duly attempted to do, but his Home Rule Bill met the combined opposition of the Conservatives and half his own Liberal Party. It is no exaggeration to say that the Irish

4

question had altered the character of British party politics. Despite the divisions among the Liberals, Gladstone refused to abandon his Irish policy. His task was made far more difficult, however, when the Irish Nationalists were riven by Parnell's fall from grace following the revelation in 1890 of the Irish leader's adultery with Mrs O'Shea, wife of one of his own MPs [Chapter 7].

Furthermore, the Ulster Protestants, conscious that they would be swamped in a united Ireland if Home Rule were to be granted, organised themselves in implacable opposition to the measure. This led to their close association with the Conservative Party from 1886 onwards. One fruit of this was the rejection in 1893 of Gladstone's second Home Rule Bill by the House of Lords, in which the Conservatives had an unassailable majority.

The Home Rule crisis stimulated two major developments within Ireland: on the one side, an intensification of Irish nationalism which identified itself with Catholicism and Gaelic (native Irish) culture; on the other, the embracing by the Ulster Protestants of combative unionism as a means of preserving their separate regional and religious identity. In 1908 the Gaelic revival culminated in the foundation of *Sinn Fein* ('Ourselves Alone'), a political party which claimed, like the Fenians, that Ireland was a free nation temporarily enslaved by the English. It sought the creation of a *Dail* (parliament) to rule Ireland in the name of its people. Another notable factor was the development of a politically-conscious Irish labour movement. A prominent figure in this was James Connolly whose objective was an Irish Socialist republic. Connolly's Marxist sympathies led him to regard the religious issue as a capitalist plot to keep the Irish working class divided; he analysed the Irish question on a class basis, describing the Irish ruling elite as servants of English imperialism.

By 1910, the year which witnessed the Liberal majority over the Unionists reduced to the barest of margins after two general elections, the situation in Ireland had become dangerously volatile. Asquith's Liberal government turned again to Home Rule as the only solution. In 1912, in a Commons evenly split between Liberals and Unionists, the government relied on the 84 Irish Nationalists to force through the third Home Rule Bill. Since the Conservatives' customary ability to veto measures passed by the Commons had been curtailed by the reform of the House of Lords in 1911, there was now nothing to stop Home Rule from from becoming law.

The Ulster Protestants reacted by swearing to the Covenant, a formal commitment to resist by any means necessary subjugation to the South. Civil war seemed imminent. Ireland had split into two armed camps, the Ulster Volunteer Force confronting the nationalist Irish Volunteers. Asquith struggled to defuse the situation and called a constitutional conference in June 1914. Reluctantly both sides agreed to consider a form of compromise; Ireland would be partitioned between the Catholic South, which would be granted Home Rule, and the Protestant North which would remain part of the United Kingdom. The parties could not agree on where the border should be drawn and the conference adjourned two weeks before the outbreak of the Great War in 1914. In order to shelve the issue and concentrate upon the war, the government placed a Home Rule bill on the statute book with a proviso that it would not be implemented until the war was won, and the exact boundaries of Northern Ireland had been agreed [Chapter 8].

It soon became evident that the suspension of the Home Rule Act had not solved the Irish problem. In April 1916, a badly-organised and poorly-supported group of Irish Nationalists seized the General Post Office in Dublin and proclaimed the Irish Republic. After days of fierce fighting, the Republicans were defeated and their ringleaders executed. The poet, W.B.Yeats, spoke of `a terrible beauty' having been born. To the Nationalists this became an inspiring concept. To the English government it was the terror rather than the beauty that they perceived.

Efforts continued throughout the period of the First World War to resolve the differences between the conflicting Irish interests, but they came to nothing. Each time talks broke down it undermined the position of those on both sides of the divide who believed that a peaceful solution was possible. By the same token, it strengthened the case of those who argued that force was the only arbiter. The Nationalist Party began to lose ground to the more extreme Sinn Feiners. In 1919 Sinn Fein defiantly set up its own Irish Parliament in Dublin. In the same year its military wing, the Irish Republican Brotherhood, reformed itself as the Irish Republican Army (IRA), dedicated to guerilla warfare against the British.

Lloyd George, the Prime Minister, responded to the IRA with coercion, most notably by forming a fearsome irregular army unit known as `the Black and Tans'. However, when it became plain that peace could not be brought to Ireland by the use of military force, Lloyd George's thoughts turned again to the idea of a constitutional settlement acceptable to both Nationalists and Unionists. He had somehow to induce them to accept partition. He offered De Valera, the Sinn Fein leader, a truce and invited him and the other Irish leaders to London to discuss the drafting of a treaty of settlement. When they duly arrived, Lloyd George shrewdly played upon the idea that he represented the last hope of a just settlement for Ireland. In December 1921, after a long, complicated, series of discussions, the parties finally signed the Irish Treaty, according Southern Ireland Dominion status as the Irish Free State, with Ulster remaining part of the United Kingdom [Chapter 9].

It was not a perfect treaty. It had been achieved in part by trickery and it left all the parties dissatisfied to some degree, as the bitter civil war that followed in Ireland soon showed. However, while it did not usher in a new era of Anglo-Irish understanding, it did mark the end of a distinctive phase in the Irish question that had begun with the Act of Union of 1800 [Chapter 10].

# Chronology of Ireland and England 1798-1922

| | |
|---|---|
| 1798 | Rebellion led by Society of United Irishmen |
| | Trial and execution of Wolfe Tone |
| 1800 | Act of Union of Great Britain and Ireland |
| 1803 | Robert Emmet executed after leading unsuccessful rising |
| 1808 | Veto scheme rejected by the Irish Catholic bishops |
| 1823 | Catholic Association founded |
| 1828 | O'Connell wins the County Clare election |
| 1829 | Catholic Emancipation Act |
| 1835 | 'Lichfield House Compact' between the Whigs and O'Connell |
| 1838 | Tithe Act |
| | Poor Law Amendment applied to Ireland |
| 1840 | Founding of Repeal Association |
| 1842 | First issue of *The Nation*, the journal of Young Ireland |
| 1843 | Declared as 'repeal year' by O'Connell |
| | Series of 'monster' meetings |
| 1844 | O'Connell imprisoned but released on appeal |
| 1845 | First reports of potato blight, onset of Great Famine |
| 1846 | Repeal of Corn Laws |
| | Robert Peel defeated |
| | Split between O'Connell and Young Ireland |
| 1847 | Death of O'Connell |
| 1848 | Unsuccessful Young Ireland rising |
| 1850 | Founding of Irish Tenant League |
| 1858 | Fenian (Irish Republican Brotherhood) movement founded |
| 1859 | Break-up of Tenant League, Fenian Brotherhood established in USA |
| 1867 | Fenian outrages in mainland Britain |
| 1868 | Gladstone becomes Prime Minister, resolved 'to pacify Ireland' |
| 1869 | Disestablishment of Church of Ireland |
| 1870 | Gladstone's first Irish land act |
| | Home Rule movement begun by Isaac Butt |
| 1873 | Defeat of Gladstone's Irish university bill |
| 1875 | C.S.Parnell elected to Parliament |
| 1877 | Parnell becomes President of Home Rule Confederation |
| 1879 | Irish National Land League founded |
| 1879-82 | 'Land war' |

| 1880 | Gladstone forms his second ministry |
| | Parnell becomes chairman of Irish Parliamentary Party |
| | Start of the 'boycotting' campaign |
| | Trial of Parnell for conspiracy |
| 1881 | Coercion acts introduced |
| | Gladstone's '3 Fs' Land Act |
| | Parnell again arrested |
| | Land League proscribed |
| 1882 | 'Kilmainham treaty' |
| | Release of Parnell |
| | Phoenix Park murders |
| 1885 | Gladstone defeated, Conservatives returned |
| | Parnell's Irish Nationalists hold balance in Commons |
| | Gladstone's conversion to Home Rule is leaked |
| 1886 | Gladstone returned to power |
| | Gladstone introduces Home Rule Bill but is defeated in Commons |
| | Liberal Party splits |
| | Beginnings of the 'Plan of Campaign' |
| 1887 | 'Parnellism and Crime' series appears in *The Times* |
| 1888 | Special commission set up to examine charges against Parnell |
| 1889 | Letters implicating Parnell in Phoenix Park murders exposed as forgeries |
| | Parnell cited as co-respondent in O'Shea divorce case |
| 1890 | Divorce-court finds Mrs O'Shea and Parnell the guilty parties |
| | Gladstone declares that he can no longer support Parnell |
| | Irish Nationalist Party abandons Parnell |
| 1891 | Parnell dies, John Redmond becomes leader of Irish MPs |
| 1893 | Gladstone's Second Home-Rule bill introduced – passes Commons, but is rejected by House of Lords, Gaelic League founded |
| 1896 | Irish Socialist Republican Party founded |
| 1899 | Foundation of Irish Literary Theatre |
| 1903 | Wyndham's Land Act |
| 1905 | Liberals return to power |
| 1908 | Radical nationalist groups amalgamate to form Sinn Fein |
| 1910 | General elections leave the Irish Nationalist MPs holding the balance in the Commons |
| | Edward Carson elected chairman of Irish Unionist Party |
| 1911 | Parliament Act ends the Lords' absolute veto |

| 1912 | Commons pass third Home Rule Bill |
| | Solemn League and Covenant sworn in Ulster |
| 1913 | Home Rule Bill defeated in Lords |
| | Ulster Volunteer Force established |
| | Irish Volunteers founded |
| 1914 | Curragh 'mutiny', Buckingham Palace constitutional conference |
| | Britain declares war on Germany |
| | Home Rule Bill becomes law, but is suspended |
| 1916 | Roger Casement arrested for gun running |
| | Easter rising in Dublin - leaders executed, Casement hanged |
| 1917 | De Valera elected as Sinn Fein president |
| 1918 | End of First World War |
| | Following general election, Sinn Fein MPs refuse to attend Westminster |
| 1919 | Sinn Fein sets itself up as an Irish Parliament |
| | Formation of IRA |
| 1920 | Black and Tans recruited to crush IRA |
| | Government of Ireland Act provides for separate parliaments in Northern and Southern Ireland |
| 1921 | Anglo-Irish treaty |
| 1922 | Irish Free State created |
| | Irish civil war ensues |

# 1 FROM REBELLION TO UNION

In 1789, the French Revolution was greeted enthusiastically by Irish radicals. [A] One organisation to which it gave rise was the Society of United Irishmen (SUI). [B] Founded in 1791 and led by Wolfe Tone, a Protestant lawyer from Dublin, the SUI was explicitly non-sectarian; both Catholics and Protestants were welcome within it. This contrasted sharply with the religious prejudices of the agrarian gangs. In Ulster fierce hostility was evident between the Catholic `Defenders' and the Presbyterian `Peep-'o-Day-Boys'. The latter organisation swiftly absorbed the other Protestant groups and formed the Orange Order, dedicated to protestant supremacy and supported by both government officials and the landlord class. [C]

The disorder in Ireland was a source of great concern to the English government. By 1793 Britain was at war with revolutionary France, and fears of French intervention in Ireland were widespread. In an effort to lessen the unrest, the government extended the vote to Irish Catholics, although they were still denied the right to sit in Parliament. This concession won over few Catholics, although the bishops did endeavour to dissuade their flock from open rebellion. [D] More significantly, the granting of the vote excited fears among the Protestants that their position was about to be undermined. The result was an intensifying of Orange aggression towards Catholics, which in turn led to a growth in the membership of the SUI. [E] When the authorities tried to suppress the Society in 1795, it went underground and sought alliance with the Defenders.

Open rebellion followed in 1798. In the North, Protestant opinion was split between the Orangemen, who helped suppress the rising, and the SUI. As a consequence, the rebellion faltered badly in the North, while gaining considerable support in the South. There the Nationalists took revenge against Protestants for Orange repression in Ulster. In June the rising was finally crushed at Vinegar Hill by government forces assisted by Orangemen. The defeated rebels were savagely treated. [F]

The 1798 rising was a decisive event in Irish history. It convinced the English government that Ireland must be brought under tighter control. They could not risk `a French Revolution' occurring in Ireland. Their solution was the Act of Union of 1800. [G] The English Prime Minister, William Pitt, made no secret that union was a necessary war measure, but he also suggested that Catholic emancipation might eventually be one of the benefits of Union. [H]

With the Act of Union on the statute book, Catholics duly looked for emancipation as the government's part of the bargain. Pitt felt morally committed to it [I], and expected George III to concede it. However, the cabinet was split on the question, which enabled the King, who claimed it contravened his coronation oath, to refuse it. Pitt thereupon resigned.[J]

As a short-term expedient the Act of Union satisfied English expectations. Despite an abortive rising led by Robert Emmet in 1803, [K] the threat of a French invasion from the West had been removed and the Protestant supremacy in Ireland had been confirmed. In the long term, however, the Union damaged Anglo-Irish relations. The eventual granting of Catholic emancipation in 1829 made the Protestants fear for their privileges. Sectarianism became an increasingly divisive factor in Irish affairs. To many Irishmen the Act of Union was the cause of Ireland's subsequent suffering. [L] The Union issue was to cast its shadow over the Anglo-Irish political scene for the next 120 years.

## A  Wolfe Tone explains the attraction of the French Revolution of 1789 for the oppressed people of Ireland

Ireland [was] an oppressed, insulted, and plundered nation. As we well knew what it was to be enslaved, we sympathised most sincerely with the French people; we had not, like England, a prejudice rooted in our very nature against France. As the Revolution advanced, and as events expanded themselves, the public spirit of Ireland rose with a rapid acceleration. The fears and animosities of the aristocracy rose in the same, or a still higher proportion. In a little time the French Revolution became the test of every man's political creed, and the nation was fairly divided into two great parties, the Aristocrats and the Democrats (epithets borrowed from France), who have ever since been measuring each other's strength, and carrying on a kind of smothered war, which in the course of events, may soon call into energy and action.

from *The Autobiography of Theobald Wolfe Tone,* edited by R. Barry O'Brien (1893)

## B  The SUI declares its aims

We have agreed to form the Society of United Irishmen, and we pledge ourselves to our country, and mutually to each other, that we will endeavour to carry into effect the following resolutions:
1st. That the weight of the English influence in the government of this country is so great, as to require a cordial union among all the people of Ireland, to maintain the balance which is essential to the preservation of our liberties, and extension of our commerce.
2nd. That the sole constitutional means by which this influence can

be opposed is by a complete and radical reform of the representation of the people in parliament.

3rd. That no reform is practicable, efficacious, or just, which shall not include Irishmen of every religious persuasion.

from *Resolutions of the United Irishmen* (1797)

### C The earlier co-operation between Catholics and Presbyterians breaks down into bitter rivalry

The North [of Ireland] was convulsed by two confederacies, Defenders and Peep-'o-day-boys. The former may be traced back to the summer of '84 and arose from an accidental quarrel betwixt a Romanist and a Presbyterian. At this time defenderism seemed to be uninfluenced by religious feelings. Both parties recruited and collected arms; 'but Presbyterians and Papists mixed indiscriminately, and were marked for some time by the district to which they belonged'.

During the American war [1776-83] some Presbyterians, who had revolutionary projects, invited the Roman Catholics to join them in arms, for the use of which they were prohibited by law.

When the restoration of peace had defeated the hopes of the Presbyterians, they resolved to disarm the Roman Catholics, who refused to surrender them, and boasted that they would not lay them down until they obtained a further extension in their privileges. Such boasting alarmed the fears of the Presbyterians, who proceeded to disarm them.

It may be imagined that two bodies would soon evince a malignity towards each other. Scarcely a night passed but some scene of violence was enacted. In their domiciliary visits, under the pretext of seeking arms, the Presbyterians destroyed the property of the Catholics and abused them inhumanly, while secret assassination was commonly resorted to by the Defenders.

While some influential landholders pandered to the passions of the opposing parties, to forward their political intrigues, others worked upon the credulity of the Romanists. Prophecies were promulgated about intended massacres to be committed by the Presbyterians; that Catholics would be remorselessly sacrificed. These terrible forebodings worked upon the excitable imaginations of the multitude. The disturbances increased till it became a downright religious war.

from *History of the Irish Rebellion in 1798,* by W.H.Maxwell (1845)

### D Archbishop Troy on improvements in Catholic status 1798

Twenty years ago the exercise of your religion was prohibited by law; the ministers were proscribed; it was penal to educate Catholic youth; your property was insecure, at the mercy of an informer; your industry was restrained by incapacity to realise the fruits of it. At present you are emancipated from these and other disabilities, under which your forefathers had laboured. You now profess your religion openly, and practise it; the ministers of your religion exercise their sacred functions under the sanction of law, which authorises Catholic teachers; a college for the education of your clergy has been erected; it is supported and endowed by parliamentary munificence; the restraints upon your industry are removed, together with the incapacity to realise the fruits of it for the benefit of your posterity. What has effected this favourable change? Your loyalty, your submission to the constituted authorities, your peaceable demeanour, your patience under long sufferings.

... You will perhaps reply, that some legal disabilities still exclude Roman Catholics from a seat or vote in Parliament ... I grant it. But is it by rebellion, insurrection, tumult, or seditious clamour on your part, that these incapacities are to be removed? Most certainly not.

from the 1798 Pastoral Address of Archbishop Troy

### E  The Society of United Irishmen grows in response to Orange strength

The Catholics of [Armagh] were exposed to the merciless attacks of an Orange faction, which was uncontrolled by the justices of the peace, and claimed to be supported by the Government. When these men found that illegal acts of magistrates were indemnified by occasional statutes, and the courts of justice shut against them by parliamentary barriers, they began to think they had no refuge but in joining the Union. Their disposition so to do were increased by finding the Presbyterians, of Belfast especially, step forward to espouse their cause and succour their distress. Wherever the Orange system was introduced, particularly in Catholic counties, it was observed that the numbers of United Irishmen increased most astonishingly. As their numbers were always greater than that of bigoted Protestants, our harvest was tenfold. We must confess, and most deeply regret, that it excited a mutual acrimony and vindictive spirit, which was opposite to the interest, and abhorrent to the feelings of the United Irishmen, and has lately manifested itself in outrages of so much horror.

from *Origin and Progress of 'United Irish' Movements* (1798)

### F  The 1798 rebellion is brutally suppressed

There was no ceremony in choosing the victims, the first to hand done well enough. They were stripped naked, tied to the triangle and their flesh cut without mercy, and though some men stood the torture to the last gasp sooner than become informers, others did not, and to make matters worse, one single informer in the town was sufficient to destroy all the United Irishmen in it.

from *Carlow in '98*, the Memoirs of William Farrell

**G  William Pitt Argues the Case for Union and Implies that Catholic Emancipation will be one of its Benefits**
Two propositions are indisputable: first, when the conduct of the Catholics shall make it safe for the government to admit them to the privileges of the established religion, such a question may be agitated in an united parliament, with much greater safety, than it could be in a separate legislature. In the second place, many of the objections which arise out of their situation would be removed, if the protestant legislature were no longer separate and local, but general and imperial ...
     What are the positive advantages that Ireland is to derive [from Union]? ... The protection which she will secure in the hour of danger, the most effectual means of increasing her commerce and improving her agriculture, the command of English capital, the infusion of English manners and industry, tending to ameliorate her condition, to accelerate the progress of internal civilisation, and to terminate those feuds and dissensions which now distract the country, and which she does not possess the power to control or extinguish.

from a speech of William Pitt (1799)

**H  The ambiguity of the English government's position**
I did not know that any conversation had passed upon the subject between them and lord Castlereagh – I mean in so official a form as to have produced such a deliberation as you have sent me the result of, and consequently without any knowledge of the sentiments of the government or bishops in Ireland, and those of my colleagues in administration, and the great lights of the English Church, it is really impossible for me to state anything upon this question that is really more than the outline of my own ideas, which I must desire you to understand are by no means settled.

from Duke of Portland to Thomas Pelham (26 March 1799)

**I  Robert Emmet, who led an unsuccessful rising in 1803, delivers his last words from the dock after being sentenced to death**
I am going to my cold and silent grave – my lamp of life is nearly extinguished – my race is run – the grave opens to receive me, and I sink into its bosom. I have but one request to make at my departure from this world: it is – the charity of its silence. Let no man write my epitaph; for as no man, who knows my motives, dare now vindicate

them, let not prejudice or ignorance asperse them. Let them rest in obscurity and peace! Let my memory be left in oblivion, and my tomb remain uninscribed, until other times and other men can do justice to my character. When my country takes her place among the nations of the earth, *then,* and *not till then,* let my epitaph be written. I have done.

## J   The key terms of the Act of Union, 1800

That the said united kingdom be represented in one and the same parliament, to be styled 'The parliament of the United Kingdom of Great Britain and Ireland' ...

That four lords spiritual of Ireland, and 28 lords temporal of Ireland, elected for life by the peers of Ireland, shall sit and vote on the part of Ireland in the house of lords, and 100 commoners shall sit and vote in the house of commons ...

That the churches of England and Ireland, be united into one protestant episcopal church, and that the doctrine, worship, discipline and government of the said united church shall be as the same are now by law established for the church of England ...

That his majesty's subjects of Great Britain and Ireland shall, from and after the first day of January 1801, be entitled to the same privileges, and encouragements and bounties on the like articles, being the growth, produce, or manufacture of either country respectively, and generally in respect of trade and navigation in all ports and places in the united kingdom and its dependencies.

from the Act of Union (1800)

## K   Pitt resigns over Catholic emancipation

Shortly after the assembling of the United Parliament in 1801, Pitt resigned, because the opposition of the King, now in old age, rendered it impossible for him to introduce a measure of emancipation, to which he considered himself morally pledged; and he even adopted the curious course of instructing his friends in Dublin to circulate among the disappointed Catholics a memorandum, in which he promised that, though not in power, everything would be done by him to establish their cause in the public favour. But when he learned that the King, on recovering from a prolonged fit of insanity, blamed him and his hateful advocacy of Catholic emancipation for the attack, Pitt wrote his Majesty a most apologetic and ebullient letter offering to abandon the question altogether; and in May, 1804, he returned to office, voluntarily pledged to never again disturb the mental equilibrium of the King by mentioning Catholic disabilities.

from *Bishop Doyle* by Michael MacDonagh (1896)

**L   Michael Davitt, a prominent Irish activist of a later generation, reflects on the baleful consequences of the Union**

Pitt and Castlereagh have been liberally abused for the destruction of the Irish Parliament. They were, it is true, the chief engineers of the transaction. They had to provide the money and guarantee the patents of `Nobility' which were to reward the venal gang who would sell the legislature rather than permit the people to share in its law-making rights and labours. The Irish landlords who held the Irish Parliament in their hands were willing traitors in this base and sordid design and theirs is the major share of the infamy belonging to this unparalleled act of corruption.

The change brought no better treatment of tenants or care for the country. They at once began to compete with an English landocracy far richer than themselves. In this spendthrift rivalry commenced the ruinous phase of Irish landlordism known as absenteeism. Evictions began for the first time on a large scale. The cost of extravagant living fell upon their unfortunate Irish tenants who had no right or protection of any kind in the soil beyond their capacity to earn whatever rent the owners' debts or rapacity caused to be placed upon the toil of a half-starved people. And it was in this way too, that the legal extortion known as `rack-rent' began in modern Ireland.

Famines came and went; distress was then, as later, of periodic occurrence; and English travellers through Ireland noted and told of the miserable hovels of the people, of their poverty, ignorance, and discontent, of the squalor of their homes, the rags and barbarism of their children, and denounced the lawlessness of a `semi-civilised' popish peasantry who battled against the `humanising spirit and character' of an enlightened English rule!

from *The Fall of Feudalism in Ireland* by Michael Davitt (1904)

# Questions

1 In what respects do sources A, B, C and D indicate disunity among the Irish in their resistance to English domination?   **(7 marks)**

2 Using sources E and F, and your own knowledge, suggest reasons for the failure of the Irish Rebellion of 1798.   **(7 marks)**

3 How far do sources G, H, J and K support the charge that the Act of Union was achieved by 'trickery and betrayal'?   **(9 marks)**

4 Of what value is source I to the historian concerned with studying the character of Irish nationalism?   **(8 marks)**

5 In the light of your own knowledge of subsequent developments, how justified would you judge Davitt's criticisms of the Union, as stated in source L, to have been?   **(9 marks)**

# 2 CATHOLIC EMANCIPATION

Pitt's failure to deliver emancipation, in return for Catholic support of the Union in 1800, made Catholic relief the major issue of Irish politics for the next 30 years. Initially, the emancipation movement was identified with a small group of aristocrats and lawyers based in Dublin and led by the veteran politician, Henry Grattan. The movement acted tentatively, loathe to provoke popular agitation or alienate the government. Grattan, who was elected to Westminster in 1805, realised that the Act of Union had changed the nature of the emancipation question; it now involved English Catholics, who historically had been excluded from public office on the grounds that their papal allegiance cast doubt on their loyalty to the English Crown. Consequently, when Grattan proposed Catholic emancipation in the Commons in 1808, he included a proviso that the Crown should have a veto over the appointment of Catholic bishops whom it might consider politically unacceptable. This was seen by the radical members of the emancipation movement as a betrayal of Catholic interests. [A] They broke away from Grattan and began to organise their own programme for achieving Catholic relief.

Prominent among this group was the lawyer, Daniel O'Connell, the man who was to dominate Irish politics for two generations. [B] His continual opposition to the veto made him influential among the parish priests and the Irish people at large. [C] By the 1820s O'Connell was in a strong enough position to found the Catholic Association. [D] Financed by the `Catholic rent', money collected from their congregations by the parish clergy, the Association set itself the task of educating the Catholic masses to understand that their economic distress was directly linked to their religious disabilities. [E - F] By 1825, the government was thoroughly alarmed by the unrest that O'Connell and his Association had created in Ireland. After an abortive attempt to prosecute him for inciting rebellion, it tried to suppress the Association. O'Connell, however, simply changed its name to preserve its legal status. [G]

In 1828, O'Connell stood in a by-election in County Clare against Vesey Fitzgerald. O'Connell calculated that as Fitzgerald was a popular landlord and sympathised with Catholic emancipation, a victory over him would have special significance. O'Connell's inspired campaigning won him the seat against all the odds. [H] The result was a stunning blow to Wellington's recently formed government. [I] The Duke proposed a relief bill to the King, [J] which was then introduced by Peel in 1829. [K]

Both Wellington and Peel had originally been strong opponents of emancipation; they changed their stance not on principle, but from fear of public disorder in Ireland following O'Connell's triumph. [L] The bill became law in April. [M] O'Connell tried to take his seat in the Commons in May, but was debarred because he refused to take the Oath of Supremacy. [N] He returned to County Clare and was re-elected unopposed in July. He eventually took his seat following a redrafting of the Supremacy Oath, which made it possible for him to swear to it.

## A The veto question

The veto had been raised publicly in 1808. In that year Lord Fingal went to London as the sole delegate of the Catholic body, bearing the annual petition to Parliament for the redress of their disabilities. It was suggested by Henry Grattan that Protestant prejudices would be largely conciliated, if they would announce in Parliament that the Catholics were willing to allow the State a Veto on their appointment as bishops. Lord Fingal consulted, not with the Catholic body of which he was the delegate, but with Dr Milner, an English Catholic bishop in London, who was the resident accredited agent of the Irish Catholic bishops, with the result that Ponsonby and Grattan were authorised to announce that the Catholics were willing to accept the Veto. The announcement was received with different feelings by different classes. The Irish gentry and the English Catholics were strongly in favour. The Irish bishops at first seemed rather inclined to show it favour; the priests received it with disapproval; but amongst the people, headed by O'Connell, it aroused feelings of indignation not unmingled with consternation.

from *Bishop Doyle* by Michael MacDonagh (1896)

## B O'Connell's opposition to the veto, 1813

Does any man imagine that the Catholic religion will prosper in Ireland if our prelates, instead of being what they are at present, shall become the servile tools of the administration? They would lose all respect for themselves, all respectability in the eyes of others. They would be degraded to the station of excisemen and the people, disgusted, would be likely to join the first enthusiastic preacher of some new form of Methodism, that might conciliate her ancient prejudices and court her still living passions. The ministerial bishops of Ireland would become a means of decatholicising the land.

from a speech by O'Connell (1813)

## C O'Connell's radicalism

My political creed is short and simple. It consists in believing that all men are entitled to civil and religious liberty, which while it emancipated the Catholics of Ireland, would protect the Protestant in France and Italy, and destroy the Inquisition in Spain. Religion is debased and degraded by human interference.

from a speech by O'Connell at Tralee (1818)

## D The aims of the Catholic Association

To forward petitions to parliament, not only on catholic emancipation, but for the redress of all local or general grievances ... To procure legal redress for all catholics, assailed or injured by Orange violence, as are unable to obtain it for themselves ... To encourage and support a liberal and enlightened press, which could readily refute the arguments of our enemies, and expose the falsehood of their calumnies upon us and our religion ... To procure for schools cheap publications by which catholic children may attain knowledge, without having their religion interfered with.

    The detail of the plan of your committee is this. That a monthly subscription should be raised throughout Ireland, to be denominated, 'The monthly catholic rent' ...

    That the Association should adopt, with the inhabitants of each parish, and if possible with the privity of the catholic clergyman, a number of persons to collect the subscriptions... That the amount expected from each individual shall not exceed one penny per month.

from the *Dublin Evening Post* (19 February 1824)

## E The receipts of the Catholic Association for 1826

| County | £ | s. | d. | County | £ | s. | d. |
|---|---|---|---|---|---|---|---|
| Antrim | 138 | 5 | 9 | Kerry | 381 | 3 | 3½ |
| Armagh | 113 | 6 | 3 | Kildare | 567 | 4 | 10½ |
| Cork | 2,824 | 13 | 10 | Kilkenny | 749 | 19 | 10 |
| Clare | 428 | 10 | 2 | King's | 549 | 3 | 3½ |
| Carlow | 239 | 9 | 5 | Leitrim | 148 | 2 | 9 |
| Cavan | 792 | 0 | 0 | Louth | 689 | 2 | 8½ |
| Donegal | 76 | 2 | 9 | Limerick | 548 | 8 | 11 |
| Down | 240 | 8 | 1½ | Longford | 168 | 7 | 1 |
| Dublin | 1,952 | 19 | 5 | Londonderry | 144 | 2 | 0 |
| Fermanagh | 72 | 17 | 8 | Meath | 604 | 14 | 5½ |
| Galway | 635 | 15 | 7½ | Monaghan | 194 | 15 | 10 |

| County | £ | s. | d. | County | £ | s. | d. |
|---|---|---|---|---|---|---|---|
| Mayo | 293 | 6 | 0½ | Tyrone | 65 | 10 | 7 |
| Queen's | 257 | 0 | 5½ | Westmeath | 526 | 19 | 9 |
| Roscommon | 166 | 7 | 0 | Wicklow | 174 | 14 | 7 |
| Sligo | 164 | 14 | 3½ | Wexford | 504 | 1 | 0 |
| Tipperary | 1,648 | 7 | 6½ | Waterford | 738 | 11 | 4½ |

from *Historical Sketches of the Catholic Association* by Thomas Wyse (1829)

### F  The growth of the Catholic Association
The priests furnished to the Association active representatives of the most potent influence in every parish in the land. They made 'the Catholic rent' a great success. This fund enabled the Association to subsidise a newspaper, to send barristers and attorneys, accompanied by reporters, to Petty Sessions Courts and Assizes to defend actions for the non-payment of tithes, or to bring local tyrants to account for deeds of unlegalised injustice. The Catholic Association, in truth, became all-powerful in the land. It was suppressed by the government in 1825, though the country was never so free from crime and outrage. O'Connell, however, revived it again with a slight alteration in its title – he called it 'The New Catholic Association' – but with identical methods and aims. 'I can drive a coach-and-six through any Act of Parliament,' the great Tribune used to say.

from *Bishop Doyle* by Michael MacDonagh (1896)

### G  O'Connell explains his strategy
It is true that as a Catholic I cannot, and of course never will, take the oaths at present prescribed to members of Parliament; but the authority which created these oaths can abrogate them, and I entertain a confident hope that, if you elect me, the most bigoted of our enemies will see the necessity of removing from the chosen representative of the people an obstacle which would prevent him from doing his duty to his King and Country.

The oath at present required by law is: 'That the Sacrifice of the Mass and the invocation of the blessed Virgin Mary and other saints as now practised in the Church of Rome are impious and idolatrous'. Of course, I will never stain my soul with such an oath. I leave that to my opponent, Mr. Vesey Fitzgerald. He has often taken that horrible oath; he is ready to take it again and asks your votes to enable him so to swear. I would rather be torn limb from limb than take it. Electors of the County Clare! choose between me, who abominates

that oath and Mr. Vesey Fitzgerald, who has sworn it full 20 times!
Return me to Parliament, and it is probable that such a blasphemous
oath will be abolished for ever. As your representative, I will try the
question with the friends in Parliament of Mr Vesey Fitzgerald. They
may send me to prison. I am ready to go there to promote the cause
of the Catholics, and of universal liberty. The discussion which the
attempt to exclude your representative from the House of Commons
must excite, will create a sensation all over Europe, and produce such
a burst of contemptuous indignation against British bigotry in every
enlightened country in the world, that the voice of all the great and
good in England ... being joined to the universal shout of the nations
of the Earth, will overpower every opposition, and render it impossible
for Peel and Wellington any longer to close the doors of the
constitution against the Catholics of Ireland.

from O'Connell's election address to the voters of County Clare (1828)

### H Vesey Fitzgerald on the importance of the Clare result
The election thank God is over, and I do feel happy in its being
terminated, notwithstanding the result. I have polled the gentry and
all the £50 freeholders – the gentry to a man. All the great interests
broke down, and the desertion has been universal. Such a scene as
we have had! Such a tremendous prospect as opens to us! The
organisation exhibited is so complete and so formidable that no man
can contemplate without alarm what is to follow in this wretched
country.

from a letter of Vesey Fitzgerald to Robert Peel (1828)

### I Peel's reaction to the County Clare result
The Clare election supplied the manifest proof of the abnormal and
unhealthy condition of the public mind in Ireland – that the sense of
a common grievance and the sympathies of a common interest were
beginning to loosen the ties which connect different classes in friendly
relations to each other. What was the evil? Not force - not violence -
not any act of which law could take cognizance. The real danger was
in the peaceable and legitimate exercise of a franchise according to
the will and conscience of the holder.

### J Fears of civil war in Ireland
We have a rebellion impending over us in Ireland, and we have in
England a Parliament which we cannot dissolve, the majority of
which is of opinion, with many wise and able men, that the remedy is
to be found in Roman Catholic emancipation. The demagogues of the

Roman Catholic Association hold in their hands at the present moment the political power and the fate of Ireland.

from Wellington's *Memorandum to the King* (1 August 1828)

### K  Robert Peel introduces the Catholic Emancipation Act in 1829
I have for years attempted to maintain the exclusion of Catholics from Parliament and the high offices of State. I do not think it was an unnatural or unreasonable struggle. I resign it in the conviction that it can be no longer advantageously maintained; from believing that there are not adequate materials, or sufficient instruments for its continuance. I yield therefore to a moral necessity which I cannot control; unwilling to push resistance to a point which might endanger the establishments which I wish to defend. Does that moral necessity exist? Is there more danger in continued resistance than in concession accompanied with measures of restriction and precaution? My object is to prove, by argument, the affirmative answer to these questions.

from a speech of Sir Robert Peel (March 1829)

### L  A supporter of emancipation comments on Peel's speech
Peel made a lame speech, but he could do no other than he did. His reasons for changing his line of conduct, as to the Catholics, were such as I had heard a thousand times urged by the friends of emancipation, and which applied to the former as to present circumstances. He stated that he had been prepared to retire from office in August last, but found that his retirement would be prejudicial to the proposed settlement; and he remained a minister, in spite of all he might suffer from the charge of insincerity. He said that the principal object of the intended measure would be the removal of all disqualification on account of religious belief. Here we gave a great shout, and indeed, we cheered our convert as much as we could.

from *Recollections of a Long Life* by John C.Hobhouse (1910)

### M The Catholic Relief Act, 1829
Be it enacted, that it shall be lawful for any person professing the Roman Catholic religion to sit or vote in either house of Parliament, upon taking the following oath: I, A.B., do sincerely promise and swear, that I will be faithful and bear true allegiance to his majesty King George the fourth, and will defend him to the utmost of my power against all conspiracies and attempts whatever, which shall be made against his person, crown or dignity ...
    Be it further enacted that it shall be lawful for persons professing

the Roman Catholic religion to vote at elections of members to serve in Parliament, and to be elected, being in all other respects duly qualified, upon taking and subscribing the oath ...

It shall be lawful for any professing Roman Catholic to hold, exercise and enjoy, all civil and military offices and places of trust and profit under his majesty; and to exercise any other franchise or civil right, except as hereinafter excepted ...

### N O'Connell attempts to take his seat in the Commons
O'Connell tendered the paper which showed that he had been sworn before the High Steward's Commissioners. Mr Ley delivered his opinion that O'Connell could take no other than the old oath, and if he refused he must withdraw.

O'Connell handed his paper over to Brougham, but the Speaker, in a decisive tone of voice and manner, repeated his order and O'Connell bowed slightly and withdrew. O'Connell stated his case at the Bar of the House. His chief argument was that under the words 'civil rights' was included the privilege of sitting in Parliament; but upon a strict interpretation of the statute I think it is only as a prospective act.

The next day O'Connell was asked if he would take the Oath of Supremacy. After looking at it a little, he said: 'I refuse to take the oath'. The Speaker told him to withdraw, and he withdrew.

from *Recollections of a Long Life* by John C.Hobhouse (1910)

# Questions

1 According to sources A-C, why did O'Connell reject the pre-1820 proposals for Catholic relief? **(7 marks)**

2 Using sources D-F and your own knowledge, explain why Catholic Emancipation became a popular cause in Ireland after 1822.
**(7 marks)**

3 Assess the value of sources G and H to the historian engaged in the study of parliamentary elections before 1832. **(9 marks)**

4 What light do sources I-L throw upon the government's reasons for introducing Catholic Emancipation in 1829? **(9 marks)**

5 Using sources M and N and your own knowledge, explain why O'Connell refused to take the Oath of Supremacy. **(8 marks)**

# 3 REFORM AND AGITATION

Repeal of the Act of Union had always been O'Connell's primary objective, [A] but as a political realist he was aware that this was unobtainable in the political climate of the 1830s. Consequently, while keeping the issue alive in his own country, at Westminster he pressed for internal reforms for Ireland. He was involved in the battle for the 1832 Reform Act, but was unable to restore the franchise to the Irish 40 shilling freeholders. He was to find that Parliament failed to distinguish between Irish and English problems. The government regarded the refusal of Irish Catholics to pay tithes to the Anglican Church as a crisis of law and order and met it with a Coercion Act in 1833 [B – C]. Meanwhile an act to reform the Irish Church divided English MPs and even the cabinet, and was amended beyond recognition. The tithe issue was not fully resolved until 1838. [D – E]

In 1835 an informal agreement between O'Connell and Lord John Russell, known as the Lichfield House Compact, resulted in Whigs, Radicals and Irish MPs combining to force Peel's minority Conservative government from office. The Irish MPs agreed to support the Whigs and drop repeal agitation in exchange for local government reforms at home. The Compact had the effect of directing O'Connell away from mass agitation into parliamentary politics. His declared aim was to `test the Union', but he was to be disappointed with the results. He could not, for example, stop the 1834 Poor Law being extended to Ireland. He argued, as did many other Irish landowners, that a Poor Law, based upon the principle of `less eligibility', was wholly inappropriate to the particular conditions of rural Ireland. [F – G]

Although the legislation for Ireland largely failed to meet nationalist expectations ,[H] there were some administrative reforms. Thomas Drummond the Irish Under-Secretary, undertook a revision of the judicial system, with a view to giving Catholics an active role within it. He hoped to convince them that the law was not simply a tool of oppression, used to maintain Protestant supremacy.

Despite such well-intended measures, by the time the Conservatives had taken power under Robert Peel in 1841 a strong conviction had developed that the Union was a sham; although constitutionally the two countries were united, English governments continued to treat Ireland as a colony. *Young Ireland,* a group of radical, non-sectarian, Irish nationalists, became prominent in the growing agitation for repeal of the Union. [I] O'Connell took up the cry. He returned to mass politics by organising the Repeal Association along lines similar to those of the successful Catholic Association of the 1820s. `Monster' meetings demanding an end to the Union became common. [N]

However, achieving emancipation in 1829 had altered the political balance in Ireland. [K] If an Irish parliament were to be restored, Catholic voters would dominate it, a prospect that struck fear into many Protestants, particularly those in Ulster. [J – M] In addition, the repeal movement was confronted by the implacable face of `Orange' Peel, who was adamant that the Union should be preserved. In October 1843, he prohibited a monster meeting planned for Clontarf. O'Connell and six others were arrested and charged with conspiracy and incitement. Convicted in February 1844, O'Connell was sentenced to one year's imprisonment and a £2,000 fine. At 70 years of age, and terminally ill, the `Liberator' could no longer lead as he had in the past. Although some nationalists adopted a conciliatory approach, [L] the *Young Ireland* movement with its uncompromising methods had begun to take over as the main expression of Irish nationalism. [Chapter 5] O'Connell lived to see the horror of famine in Ireland, but in February 1847 he died in Italy while on a pilgrimage to Rome.

### A  O'Connell's hatred of the Act of Union

We have been robbed of our birthrights, our independence. England that ought to have been a sister and a friend – whom we had loved, and fought and bled for – stole upon us like a thief in the night and robbed us of the precious gem of our liberty ...

The real cause of the Union is the religious dissensions which the enemies of Ireland have created, separating us into wretched sections. They belied and calumniated us to one another. They falsely declared that we hated each other. And they continued to repeat the assertion until we came to believe it. They succeeded in producing the madness of party and religious dissension and plundered us of our country ... Learn discretion from your enemies. They have crushed your country by fomenting discord - serve her by abandoning it for ever. I trample under foot the Catholic claims if they can interfere with the Repeal of the Union.

from a speech by O'Connell (1809)

### B  Agitation against tithes

The efforts of the Protestant clergy or their agents to collect tithes by seizing farm produce was generally met by passive resistance. It was not legal to break open a door in order to get at the stock or chattels of a defaulting tithe payer. Scouts were constantly on the watch for the approach of a raiding party; and when that was announced, the cattle were hurriedly placed under lock and key. But if the cow or the crops or the household furniture, were seized and put up for auction, no one bought. In some cases the resistance was not passive but active. At Newtownbarry a conflict took place in 1831 between the people and the forces of the Crown, in which several peasantry were killed. At Carrishock in the same year, the people, armed with scythes and pitchforks attacked a force of police, accompanying some process-servers, utterly routed them, and killed 18 of the force, including the commanding officer.

from *Bishop Doyle* by Michael MacDonagh (1896)

### C  The failure of the tithe system
It had become impossible to collect tithe in Ireland; and to collect would never be possible again. Here was the insulted Church to be vindicated – for there was as yet no debate whether to maintain it – and the starving Irish clergy to be succoured; many of whom had pawned or sold their furniture and clothes, and were working like labourers to raise potatoes to feed their children, or were thankful for the gift of a meal of porridge for their families from a neighbour.

from *A History of the Thirty Years Peace* by Harriet Martineau (1877)

### D  The reform of the Irish Church 1833
Lord Althorp told me of the plan to be proposed for Irish Church Reform, and said he expected it would be received with acclamation. Well might he say this! Ten bishops were to be abolished; Church cess [taxes] given up; and Church revenues revised and distributed. I heard Althorp open his Church of Ireland Reform scheme. He was quite right; it was hailed with acclamation. There were thunders of applause, O'Connell and the Irish particularly loud. O'Connell expressed his gratitude to ministers publicly.

from *Recollections of a Long Life* by Lord Broughton (1968)

### E  English opposition to Irish Church reform 1833
Following the Coercion Act, one million sterling was advanced to the parsons in compensation for the tithes unpaid for three years, amounting to the enormous figure of £3,250,000; and `The Church Temporalities Act' was passed. The Bill as originally introduced, contained `the appropriations clause', proposing to apply the surplus revenues of the Church to secular purposes for the benefit of the country. But this clause, which was the main recommendation of the Bill in the eyes of the Irish people, met with such opposition in both Houses (and even in the Cabinet, from Stanley, the Irish Chief

Secretary) that it had to be dropped. `The Church Temporalities Act' did very little to relieve the burden of tithes. It was not until 1838 that the `Tithe Commutation Act' (the fifth bill to be introduced between 1834 and 1838) was passed, after a determined struggle with the Lords. The Act transformed the impost into a rent-charge, fixed at 75 per cent of the existing tithe – the deduction of 25 per cent being for the cost of collection – and payable by the landlords.

from *Bishop Doyle* by Michael MacDonagh (1896)

### F The debate on the proposed Irish Poor Law

a) Ireland stands in need of a system of poor laws based upon that principle fully as much as England itself. In every instance but one, I have found the Catholic hierarchy disposed heartily to concur in all that I propose. [I] have also gone amongst the people, into their cabins - in the markets, into the fields and I found a similar feeling to prevail with them. [It] would not give employment or capital, but it would, I think help the country through what may be called its transition period, from the system of small-holdings... and the sub-divisions of land to the better practice of day-labour for wages.

from a letter of George Nicholls to Lord Russell (October 1836)

b) To adopt any plan undertaking the relief of the *able-bodied* poor of Ireland will strike a blow at the whole social system of the country industry, retard civilisation and introduce an uncertainty with respect to all property. It supplies the only element of mischief from which we have hitherto been protected.

from a memorandum by Thomas Spring-Rice to Lord Russell (November 1836)

### G Irish Poor Law proposals – an Irish gentry view 1837

Write and tell me how you like Mr Nicholl's late report on poor laws for Ireland. I hope you will not tell me I am wrong in esteeming it. I was much averse to *any* poor law for Ireland. On the principle of non-interference of legislative enactions between landlord and tenant, industry and its wages, idleness and its punishment, overpopulation and its consequences, I deprecated the measure altogether. But Mr Nicholl's report has brought me to the belief that the workhouse system which he proposes, guarded by the destitution test, may be *safely* tried in Ireland and that the probability of its advantages to this country far outweigh the expense of the experiment. It is not in human power to do the work of time and to carry any country suddenly through what Nicholl well calls the transition state with its

27

necessary attendant evils, but whatever *can* be done by legislative aid
this measure will effect. In short Mr N. seems to me to have solved
the problem of doing with the least chance of mischief the greatest
chance of good by a poor law to Ireland.

from Maria Edgeworth to Revd Richard Jones (April 1837)


**H O'Connell appeals for further concessions**
Why does not Lord John [Russell] treat us to an epistle declaratory of
his determination to abate the Church nuisance in Ireland, to
augment our popular franchise, to vivify our new corporations, to
mitigate the statute law as between landlord and tenant, to strike off a
few more rotten boroughs in England, and to give the representatives
to our great counties? Why does he not prove himself a high-minded
statesman, capable of conciliating the Irish nation, and strengthening
the British Empire?

from O'Connell to Lord Campbell (September 1843)


**I Young Ireland denounces the Whig Reforms**
Modern Anglicism – i.e. Utilitarianism, the creed of Russell and Peel,
as well as of the Radicals – which measures prosperity by
exchangeable value, measures duty by gain, and limits desires to
clothes, food, and respectability – this damned thing has come into
Ireland under the Whigs, and is equally the favourite of the `Peel'
Tories. It is believed in the political assemblies of our cities, preached
from our pulpits (always Utilitarian or persecuting); it is the very
Apostles' Creed of the professions, and threatens to corrupt the lower
classes, who are still faithful and romantic. To use every literary and
political engine against this seems to me the first duty of an Irish
patriot who can foresee consequences. This is a greater though not so
obvious danger as papal supremacy. So much worse that, sooner
than suffer the iron gates of that filthy dungeon to close on us, I
would submit to the certainty of a papal supremacy.

from John Dillon to Daniel Owen Maddyn (July 1842)


**J Protestant denunciations of concessions to Irish nationalism**
What would be the feelings of the noble lord, the Secretary for
Ireland, if I presumed to propose for England a measure such as that
which he has dared to suggest should be established in Ireland? We
are very much dissatisfied in Ireland. We want English legislation in
Ireland. We ask you to govern Ireland as you do England, or we shall
remain in agitation.

from a speech of Lord Clements (1843)

## K The condition of Ireland after emancipation

Political changes [had been] accomplished – Catholics were
emancipated and Parliament was reformed – but the system on which
Ireland was governed had undergone no substantial change. Every
institution and agency was still strictly Protestant. The judiciary,
executive, and local magistracy were Protestant in the proportion of
more than a 100 to one. Half the rural population were steeped in
habitual misery. The great estates were held by English absentees,
who ruled the country from Westminster, mainly for their own profit
and security. The resident gentry were for the most part their
dependants or adherents, entrenched behind a standing army. The
country sent a few national and a few Catholic representatives to the
Imperial Parliament, but the franchise was so skilfully adjusted, that in
Dublin a citizen had sometimes to pay as many as 10 separate rates
and taxes before he became entitled to vote. The one powerful tribune
[O'Connell] constantly demanded in Parliament and on the popular
platform the rights withheld from the people. He had against him the
Irishmen controlling public opinion. [His] sincerity was doubted
because he impaired the national claim by coupling it with a radical
reform of the House of Commons, revision of the land code, and the
abolition of tithe – questions to be dealt with by the Imperial
Parliament.

O'Connell had laid himself open to a suspicion among men of
public spirit. He had pulled down the banner of nationality, in order to
grasp the patronage of the government. He could doubtless plead in
defence that he had brought into power the Irish administration of
Mulgrave and Drummond, and raised O'Loghlen and Woulfe to the
bench.

In 1840 the government which he had supported fell from power,
and he immediately took up the national question anew.

from *A Short Life of Thomas Davis* by Gavan Duffy (1895)

## L Nationalists claim that a restored Irish parliament would unite all Irishmen

Nationality is the first great object which will not only raise our people
from their poverty, by securing to them the blessings of a DOMESTIC
LEGISLATURE, but inflame and purify them with a heroic love of
country, to be stamped on our manners, literature, and deeds, which
may embrace Protestant, Catholic and Dissenter, the Irishman of a
hundred generations and the stranger within our gates; not a
nationality which would prelude civil war but which would establish
internal union and external independence; which would be recognised
by the world, and sanctified by wisdom, virtue and prudence.

from *The Nation* (July 1842)

## M Irish Protestant separatism in the 1840s

Belfast still claimed to be the chief seat of liberality and letters in the island, but the `Athens of Ireland' [was] as ugly and sordid as Manchester; its temples hideous Little Bethels, its orators noisy fanatics, and the old historic spirit soured into bigotry worthy of Rochelle, the Belfast of France. The Belfast Whigs were Protestant liberals, in general sympathy with the English Whigs, but a genuine nationalist was nearly unknown among them. The Catholic bishop and clergy to whom I presented my friend saw for the first time an Irish Protestant who recognised the old race as the natural spokesman of public opinion, who sympathised passionately with the historic memories of which they were proud, but never forgot that the Protestant minority were equally Irishmen.

from *A Short Life of Thomas Davis* by Gavan Duffy (1895)

## N O'Connell arouses his Irish audience

Gentlemen, I think I perceive a fixed disposition on the part of our Saxon traducers to put us to the test. In the midst of peace and tranquillity they are covering our land with troops. As long as they leave us a rag of the Constitution we will stand on it. We will violate no law, we will assail no enemy; but you are much mistaken if you think others will not assail you ...

What are Irishmen that they should be denied an equal privilege? Have we not the ordinary courage of Englishmen? Are we to be called slaves? Are we to be trampled under foot?

Cromwell, the only Englishman who ever possessed Ireland, sent 80,000 Irishmen to work as slaves beneath the ungenial sun of the Indies. Peel and Wellington may be second Cromwells. They may enact Cromwell's massacre of the women of Wexford. But by God they never shall. *[Tremendous cheering and waving of handkerchiefs by the ladies.]*Remember that deed. When Cromwell entered the town, 300 inoffensive women, of all ages and classes were collected around the Cross of Christ, erected in the the Bull Ring. They prayed to Heaven for mercy. They prayed to the English for humanity and Cromwell slaughtered them. *[Cries of `Oh! Oh!' and a great sensation, and many of the ladies screaming with terror.]* But there is no danger to the women of Ireland, for the men of Ireland would die to the last in their defence. *[Wild cheering, the entire company on its feet.]* We were a paltry remnant in Cromwell's time. We are nine million now!

from a speech by O'Connell at a monster meeting (1843)

# Questions

**1** What similarities and what differences of attitude between O'Connell and *Young Ireland* towards Irish nationalism are detectable in sources A, I and N? **(7 marks)**

**2** Using your own knowledge and sources B-E, indicate why the tithe question was such a contentious issue in Anglo-Irish relations. **(8 marks)**

**3** In the light of sources F and G, consider the political and economic implications of the Irish Poor Law of 1838. **(8 marks)**

**4** From your own knowledge and with reference to sources H, K and M, consider the view that by the 1840s it was clear that the Act of Union had `failed the test'. **(8 marks)**

**5** In what ways do sources J, L and M illustrate the complexity of Irish reaction to the Whig reforms of the 1830s? **(9 marks)**

# 4 FAMINE

At the start of the 1840s the Irish economy was in a very weak condition. Most of the population, which had doubled since the beginning of the previous century, lived on the land on plots too small for much more than subsistence potato farming. Eviction for non-payment of rent meant destitution. In order to pay rents tenants frequently subdivided their holdings; by 1845 a large number of Irish people lived a precarious life on plots of less than one acre, on which they grew potatoes and perhaps kept a pig. Inefficient and archaic though the system was, it did sustain the population through the first four decades of the century, albeit at a precarious level. [A – C]

It was the unexpected arrival in Europe of the fungus, *phythophthera infestans,* in 1845 which destroyed the potato crop in Ireland and created the Great Famine, an experience which was to dominate Irish history for the rest of the century. Potato-crop failure was not unprecedented; blight was recurrent in Ireland. However, it had rarely come in successive years. The middle 1840s were different; the survival of the fungus in the soil and the repetition of weather conditions ideal for its spread meant that the first total crop failure in 1845 was followed by a second in 1846 and a third in 1847.

The disaster was on such a scale that it was probably beyond the resources of any government to avert. [D – E] Nevertheless, the response of the English government appeared to make things worse. The prevailing economic orthodoxy of *laissez-faire,* which emphasised minimal government interference with the pattern of supply and demand, inhibited English officials from responding to the events in Ireland. [F] A further constraint on government action was the New Poor Law, the utilitarian principles of which discouraged the immediate distribution of relief. [G – H] Reinforcing this reluctance to act was the perception, widely held among the English ruling class, of the Irish peasantry as feckless and, therefore, responsible for their own misery. [I]

The impression of government indifference to famine in Ireland left a bitter legacy. Even those with a vested interest in the existing landlord system were deeply affected by the suffering they witnessed. [J and K] Government action was directed by C.E. Trevelyan, the Assistant Secretary to the Treasury. He was more concerned with avoiding an increase in public expenditure, than with alleviating suffering. Trevelyan went so far as to suggest `too much has been done for the people'.

The failure of government policy in Ireland in the late 1840s should not obscure the self-sacrifice and concern of private individuals, many of whom made prodigious efforts to save others. However, the predominant Irish perception was that the severity of the famine was the product of English indifference, landlord obstinacy, and the complicity of Irishmen in their own destruction. Such perception fuelled the more violent and militant nationalism that developed in the second half of the 19th century. [L – N]

The Great Famine had profound effects on Ireland and on Anglo-Irish relations. There was a dramatic drop in the population of Ireland; caused initially by the million deaths directly resulting from the famine. It was compounded by a flood of emigrations to mainland Britain, the dominions, and the USA. The famine also began a decline of landlordism and saw the emergence of a new policy by which eventually a system of peasant proprietorship was created. In English politics it was instrumental in bringing about the repeal of the Corn Laws. Perhaps most importantly, it confirmed the Irish nationalists in their belief that the major cause of their troubles was English domination of Ireland, a situation that could be remedied only by the expulsion of the oppressor. [Chapters 6 and 7]

## A  Irish Population in the 19th Century

| | | | |
|---|---|---|---|
| 1804 | 5,400,000 | 1861 | 5,799,000 |
| 1813 | 5,937,000 | 1871 | 5,412,000 |
| 1821 | 6,801,000 | 1881 | 5,175,000 |
| 1831 | 7,767,000 | 1891 | 4,705,000 |
| 1841 | 8,175,000 | 1901 | 4,458,000 |
| 1851 | 6,552,000 | | |

## B  The pre-famine pattern of peasant land holding

A family in the West of Ireland, once located on from one to three or four acres,was provided for; a cabin could be raised in a few days without the expense of a sixpence [2½p]; the potatoes supplied a sufficiency of food, with which, from habit, they were perfectly content; and a pig, and occasional labour at a very low rate of wages, gave them what was necessary to pay rent, and for such clothing and other articles as were absolutely necessary, and which were on the lowest scale of human existence. The foundation of the whole, however, was the possession of a bit of land; it was the one, and the only one thing absolutely necessary; the rent consequently was high, and generally well paid, being the first demand on all money received, in order to secure that essential tenure; and only what remained became applicable to other objects. Although of the lowest grade, it was an easy mode of subsistence, and led to the encouragement of early marriages, large families, and a rapidly increasing population, and at the same time afforded the proprietor very good return of profit for his land.

from a letter from Sir John Burgoyne to *The Times* (6 October 1847)

### C Potato-dependency in Ireland
A population, whose ordinary food is wheat and beef, can retrench in periods of scarcity, and resort to cheaper kinds of food. But those who are entirely fed on potatoes, live on the extreme verge of human subsistence, and when they are deprived of their accustomed food, there is nothing cheaper to which they can resort. They have already reached the lowest point, and there is nothing beyond but starvation and beggary ...

The potato does not last even a single year. The old crop becomes unfit for use in July, and the new crop does not come into consumption until September. Hence July and August are called the `meal months', from the necessity of living upon meal at that period. This is always a season of great distress for the poorer peasants; and in the districts in which the potato system has been carried to the greatest extent there has been an annual dearth for many years past. Every now and then a `meal year' occurs, and masses of the population become a prey to famine and fever ...

The agrarian code is at perpetual war with the laws of God and man, the primary object being to secure the plots of land, which are the sole means of subsistence.

from `The Irish Crisis' by C.E.Trevelyan in *The Edinburgh Review* (January 1848)

### D A land agent describes the onset and effect of the potato blight
On 1 August, I was startled by hearing a rumour that all the potato fields in the district were blighted. I immediately rode up to visit my crop; but I found it as luxuriant as ever, and promising a splendid produce. On coming down from the mountain, I rode into the lowland country, and there I found the leaves of the potatoes on many fields were quite withered, and a strange stench, which became a well-known feature in `the blight', filled the atmosphere.

The next day I found the disease was fast extending, and on rooting up some of the potato bulbs under the withered stalks, that decay had set in, and the potato was rapidly blackening and melting away. The stench was the first indication of disease, and the withered leaf followed in a day or two. Much alarm now prevailed. Those, like me, who had staked a large amount of capital on the crop, became extremely uneasy; whilst the poorer farmers looked on helplessly at the disappearance of all they counted on for food ...

On 6 August I rode up as usual to my mountain property, and my feelings may be imagined when before I saw the crop, I smelt the fearful stench which came up from the luxuriant crop; no perceptible change, except the smell, had as yet come upon the apparent prosperity of the deceitfully luxuriant stalks, but the experience of the past few days taught me that the crop was utterly worthless ...

General desolation, misery, and starvation now rapidly affected the poorer classes throughout Ireland. It is true that in the more cultivated districts of the midland counties not many deaths occurred from actual starvation. I mean, that people were not found dead on the roads or in the fields from sudden deprivation of food; but they sank gradually from impure and insufficient diet; and fever, dysentery, the crowding in the workhouse or hardship on the relief works, carried thousands to a premature grave. The crop on which they depended for food, had suddenly melted away, and no adequate arrangements had been made to meet this calamity.

from *Realities of Irish Life* by W.Steuart Trench (1868)

### E  An Irish child's experience of the famine

The potatoes had grown to a fairly large size. But the seed of death and decay had been planted in them. They were dug and put into a pit in the field. By and by an alarming rumour ran through the country that the potatoes were rotting in the pits. Our pit was opened, and there, sure enough, were some of the biggest potatoes half rotten. The ones that were not touched with the rot were separated, and carted into the `chamber' house, back of our dwelling house that had been specially prepared for them, the walls of it being padded with straw, but soon the potatoes were rotting in the chamber too. Then all hands were set to work to make another picking; the potatoes that were rotting were thrown into the backyard, and those that were were whole and appeared sound were taken up into the loft over our kitchen. But the potatoes rotted in the loft also, and before many weeks the blight had eaten up the supply that was to last the family for a whole year.

Then one of our fields had a crop of wheat, and when the wheat was reaped and stacked, the landlord put `keepers' on it and on all we had, and these keepers remained in the house till the wheat was threshed and bagged, and taken to the mill. I well remember one of the keepers going with my mother to Lloyd's mill and from the mill to the agent who was in town that day to receive rents.

My mother came home without any money. The rent was £18 a

year. The wheat came to £18 5s and she gave all to the agent.

from *Rossa's Recollections 1838-98* by Jeremiah O'Donovan Rossa (1898)


### F  The government's initial reaction to the news of famine
On the first appearance of the blight in the autumn of 1845, Professors Kane, Lindley and Playfair, were appointed by Sir Robert Peel to inquire into the nature of it, and to suggest the best means of preserving the stock of potatoes. The result showed that the mischief lay beyond the knowledge and power of man.

The next step was to order from the United States of America £100,000 worth of Indian corn. It was considered that the void might be filled by the least disturbance of private trade and market prices, by the introduction of a new popular food. Owing to the prohibitory duty, Indian corn [maize] was unknown as an article of consumption in the United Kingdom. Private merchants, therefore, could not complain of interference with a trade which did not exist, nor could prices be raised against the home consumer on an article of which no stock was to be found in the home market. Nevertheless, with a view to avoid as long as possible, the doubts and apprehensions which must have arisen if the government had appeared as a purchaser in a new class of operations, pains were taken to keep the transactions secret, and the first cargoes from America had been more than a fortnight in Cork harbour before it became generally known.

from 'The Irish Crisis' by C.E.Trevelyan in *The Edinburgh Review* (January 1848)


### G  Attempts at providing relief
As the labouring class in Ireland had hitherto subsisted on potatoes grown by themselves, and money-wages were almost unknown, it was necessary to adopt some means of giving the people a command over the new description of food. This was done by establishing a system of public works, in accordance with the previous practice on similar occasions, both in Ireland and in other countries.

These works, which consisted principally of roads, were undertaken, and the expense of executing them was defrayed by advances of public money, half of which was a grant, and half a loan to be repaid. The largest number of persons employed in this first season of relief was 97,000 in August 1846 ...

The new and more decisive failure of the potato crop called for great exertions from Lord John Russell's newly formed government ... The system of public works was renewed. In order to check the exorbitant demands which had been made during the preceding season, the whole of the expense was made a local charge, and the advances were directed to the rate levied according to the Poor Law valuation. It was also determined that the wages given on the relief works should be somewhat below the average rate in the district; and that the persons employed should as far as possible, be paid by task or in proportion to the work actually done by them; and that the Relief Committee, instead of giving tickets entitling persons to employment on the public works, should furnish lists of persons requiring relief, which should be carefully revised by the Board of Works; the experience of the preceding season having shown that these precautions were necessary to confine the relief works to the destitute, and to enforce a reasonable quantum of work.

from `The Irish Crisis' by C.E.Trevelyan in *The Edinburgh Review* (January 1848)

### H Relief proves inadequate
It is said that numbers who have been employed in public works are so much weakened that they cannot work without being supplied with food. *Spite* of all the soup shops and charity it is come to this. *Spite of all*, I say. I could not venture to say in *consequence* of the gratis [free] feeding, because there must be an exception to the general rule 'If thou dost not work, thou shalt not eat', for here it has been: 'Even if thou dost work, thou shalt not eat'. Here is a national calamity by the hand of God, inflicted no doubt for wise purpose, but which all the wisdom of men cannot avert or remedy completely.

The quantity of provisions that have been sent over to Ireland to be locked up in stores till certain time or certain prices prevailed and have been wasted and spoiled when opened, is lamentable! Also the quantity of money that has been wasted and is now wasting in paying officers, watching officials, hundreds per annum to oversee draining and other works of which they (the overseers) are perfectly ignorant, is also lamentable. It is surprising how clearly the common people and the very lowest Irish labourer sees these blunders. 'Sure!' said our under gardener, who by the way cannot *write.* 'Sure, the half of the fifteen hundred a year that's spent in this country on them Englishmen teaching us how to drain, which we know well enough, would have bought meal enough to have fed them all that has died of hunger and *is* perishing still'.

from a letter of Maria Edgeworth to Fanny Edgeworth (March 1847)

### I The Irish viewed as responsible in part for their own misery
Alas! the famine progresses; here it is in frightful reality to be seen in every face. Idle, improvident, reckless, meanly, dependent on the

upper classes whom they so abuse, call the bulk of the Irish what we will and no name is too hard almost for them, here they are starving round us, cold, naked, hungry, well nigh houseless. To rouse them from their natural apathy may be the work of future years. To feed them must be our business, this [year].

Discovered another feature in the overwhelming distress of the times – the relief don't reach down to the very lower classes it was intended principally to succour. Most of the labourers are in debt – a week's provisions is the ordinary extent.

The relief now afforded at a great expense is but a mockery – one pound of dry meal a day to adults, half a pound to children without any sort of kitchen; it may keep them alive a few weeks, but in the end a pestilence must ensue; the quantity is not sufficient and the quality is defective ...

Death and starvation in Ireland at any rate, progressing rapidly. The roads are crowded with wretched beggars from the south and west, famine too truly depicted on their miserable skeletons, hardly concealed by rags.

from the journals of Elizabeth Smith (1846)


## J  A land agent describes the shortcomings of individual charity

There was abundance of corn and meal within some few miles of the district [Schull], and no lack of funds to purchase these provisions; and yet in proximity to this plenty, the people were dying by hundreds, of actual dire starvation, merely for want of someone with sufficient energy and powers of organisation *to bring the food and the people together.* In one place a most benevolent clergyman, having obtained large funds from England to mitigate the famine, appeared in the morning at his own hall door, and threw handfuls of shillings and sixpences amongst the crowd who had collected to receive charity. Amiable gentleman no doubt he was, and most honourable in the distribution of all he had received; but he forgot that starving people could not eat sixpences or shillings, and the food was some 10 miles off. The people had no strength nor energy to seek, purchase, or cook meal or flour, and with silver in their hands they died.

from *Realities of Irish Life* by W.Steuart Trench (1868)


## K  A defence of the landlords

The cry against Irish landlords, which has been unjust, will be completely put down by the humanity and most active exertions of the landed proprietors during the distress in Ireland. It is not fair to argue either as to good or bad from a few instances, but it is fair to take them into account. I could name at least ten or twelve great landed proprietors who have this season and last year lost their lives from overexertion and from fever caught in attending their tenants and the poor. And Protestant clergymen in great numbers have so zealously exerted themselves that they have won the affection of the *poor* Catholics and even their priests, convinced that they have not used any undue means of *conversion* are much conciliated. This is a *good* which will survive the evil.

from a letter of Maria Edgeworth to Fanny Edgeworth (March 1847)

## L  Young Ireland's perception of the famine

... A people whose lands and lives are in the keeping and custody of others, instead of in their own, are not in a position of common safety. The Irish famine is example and proof. The corn crops were sufficient to feed the island. But the landlords would have their rents in spite of famine and in defiance of fever. They took the whole harvest and left hunger to those who raised it. Had the people of Ireland been the landlords of Ireland not a single human creature would have died of hunger, nor the failure of the potato been considered a matter of any consequence.

from a letter of James Fintan Lalor to *The Irish Felon* (June 1848)

## M  An Irishman's view of the landlord's role in the famine

The landlords made a raid upon the grain crops and sold them for their rents, leaving the producers of those crops to starve or perish or fly the country. Thousands of families were broken up; thousands of homes were razed. People now allude to those years as the 'famine' in Ireland. There was no 'famine' in Ireland; there is no famine in any country that will produce in any one year as much food as will feed the people who live in that country. In 1845 there were 9,000,000 people in Ireland; allowing that the potato crop failed, other crops grew well, and the grain and cattle grown in the country were sufficient to sustain three times 9,000,000 people. England and the agents of England seized those supplies of food, and sent them out of the country, and then raised the cry that there was 'famine' in the land. There was no famine, but plunder of the Irish people by the English government of Ireland; and the Coroner's juries, called upon to give judgement in cases of people found dead had brought in verdicts of 'murder' against the English government.

from *Rossa's Recollections 1838-98* by Jeremiah O'Donovan Rossa (1898)

## N A Fenian's interpretation of the famine

There is possibly no chapter in the wide records of human suffering
so full of shame – measureless, unadulterated, sickening shame as
that which tells us of 200,000 adult men lying down to die in a land
out of which 45 millions' worth of food was being exported, in one
year alone, for rent - the product of their own toil – and making no
effort, combined or otherwise, to assert even the animal's right of
existence – the right to live by the necessities of its nature. It stands
unparalleled in human history, with nothing approaching to it in the
complete surrender of all the ordinary attributes of manhood by

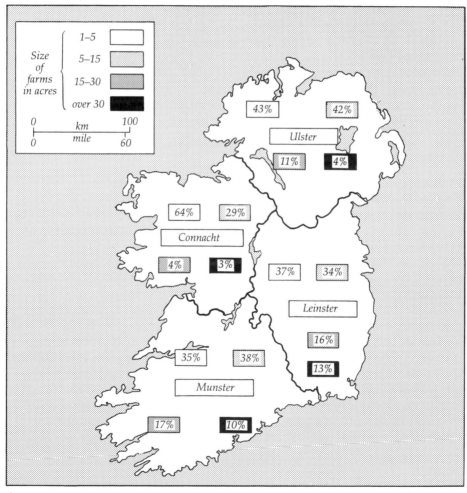

**The Structure of post-famine agriculture in Ireland**

almost a whole nation, in the face of artificial famine.

from *The Fall of Feudalism in Ireland* by Michael Davitt (1904)

# Questions

1 What insights into the condition of the Irish peasantry on the eve of the Famine are offered by sources A-C? **(7 marks)**

2 In the light of the evidence in sources D and E, examine the nature and scale of the potato blight that struck Ireland in the mid-1840s. **(7 marks)**

3 Using your own knowledge and the evidence in sources F-I, examine the factors which prevented adequate famine relief being provided. **(10 marks)**

4 Which source paints the more convincing picture of the role of Irish landlords in the famine, source J or K? **(8 marks)**

5 Assess the value of sources L-N to historians engaged in the study of the effects of the famine. **(8 marks)**

# 5 ANGLO-IRISH RELATIONS

## ILLUSTRATED

**The Irish House of Commons, 1790-1800, often known as Grattan's Parliament, abolished by the Act of Union**

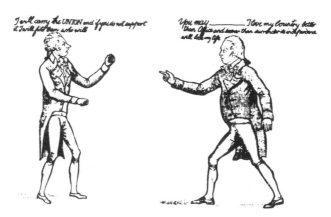

**A cartoon depicting Pitt, the British Prime Minister, trying to overcome opposition within his Government to the Union**

`Misther Shpeaker, Sorr, wid the greatest re-spekt, Sorr'; the cartoon and caption represent the mocking view of the archetypal Irish MP held by many English people in the 19th century

A print showing Daniel O'Connell addressing one of his Monster meetings

# NOTICE.

WHEREAS, there has appeared, under the Signatures of " E. B. Sugden, C., Donoughmore, Eliot, F. Blackburne, E. Blakeney, Fred. Shaw, T. B. C. Smith," a paper being, or purporting to be, a PROCLAMATION, drawn up in very loose and inaccurate terms, and manifestly misrepresenting known facts ; the objects of which appear to be, to prevent the PUBLIC MEETING, intended to be held TO-MORROW, the 8th instant, at CLONTARF, *to petition Parliament* for the REPEAL of the baleful and destructive measure of the LEGISLATIVE UNION.

AND WHEREAS, such Proclamation has not appeared until *late in the Afternoon of this Saturday, the 7th*, so that it is utterly impossible that the knowledge of its existence could be communicated in the usual Official Channels, or by the Post, in time to have its contents known to the Persons intending to meet at CLONTARF, for the purpose of Petitioning, as aforesaid, whereby ill-disposed Persons may have an opportunity, under cover of said Proclamation, to provoke Breaches of the Peace, or to commit Violence on Persons intending to proceed peaceably and legally to the said Meeting.

WE, therefore, the COMMITTEE of the LOYAL NATIONAL REPEAL ASSOCIATION, do most earnestly request and entreat, that all well-disposed persons will, IMMEDIATELY on receiving this intimation, repair to their own dwellings, and no place themselves in peril of any collision, or of receiving any ill-treatment whatsoever.

And We do further inform all such persons, that without yielding in any thing to the unfounded allegations in said alleged Proclamation, we deem it prudent and wise, and above all things humane, to DECLARE that said

## Meeting is abandoned, and is not to be held.

Signed by Order,

# DANIEL O'CONNELL,

Chairman of the Committee.

## T. M. RAY, Secretary.

*Saturday, 7th October,* 1843.
3 *o'Clock* P. M.

RESOLVED—That the above Cautionary Notice be immediately transmitted by Express to the Very Reverend and Reverend Gentlemen who signed the Requisition for the CLONTARF MEETING, and to all adjacent Districts, SO AS TO PREVENT the influx of Persons coming to the intended Meeting.

## GOD SAVE THE QUEEN.

Browne, Printer, 36, Nassau-street.

**In response to pressure from Peel's government, O'Connell calls off a monster meeting scheduled for Clontarf**

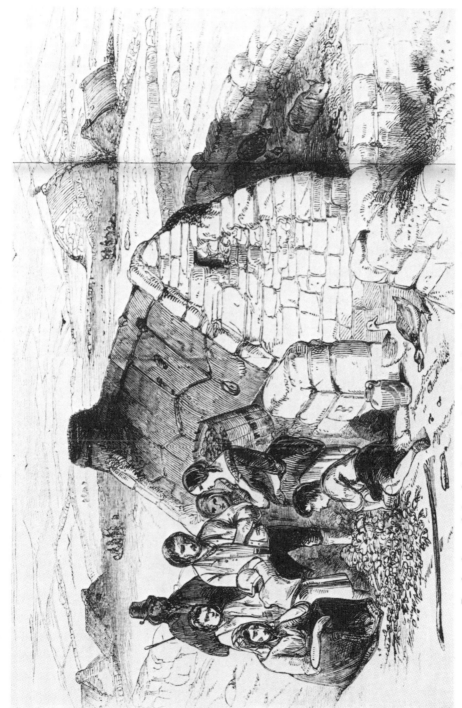

**Beginnings of the famine; a print depicting the failure of the potato crop in 1845**

Desperate searching for edible potatoes in the putrefying crop; from the *Illustrated London News,* 1849

**The Famine meant that large numbers of tenants could not pay their rents; eviction invariably followed (from the *Illustrated London News*)**

**Many desperate victims tried to escape the famine by emigrating to North America; conditions on board were often so grim that the vessels were known as coffin ships. The scene shows Liverpool docks (from the *Illustrated London News*)**

## THE ENGLISH LABOURER'S BURDEN;

### OR, THE IRISH OLD MAN OF THE MOUNTAIN.

`The English Labourer's Burden' – a *Punch* cartoon suggesting that English workers were having to bear the cost of famine relief in Ireland

Fenians ambush a prison van in Manchester in 1867. Following the total
failure of the Fenian rising in Ireland in that year, the campaign was
carried to the English mainland for the first time

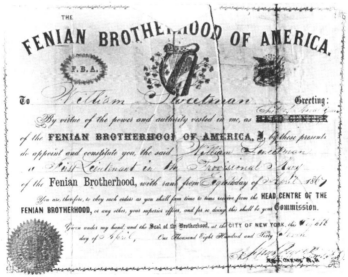

A membership card of 'The Fenian Brotherhood of America', 1867. An
abortive invasion of Canada was attempted by the American Fenians in
the hope that it would incite a war between the USA and Britain and
thus advance the cause of Irish independence

A Fenian bomb attack on Clerkenwell prison in London in 1867 blew
down the outer wall, killing thirty civilians

THE EXECUTION OF BARRETT.

The execution of a Fenian in 1868

LANDLORDISM ON THE HORNS OF A DILEMMA.

**A Land League cartoon suggesting that its 'Plan of Campaign' was successful in forcing landlords into the impossible position of having to choose between coercion and conciliation**

LAND LEAGUE CRUELTY.

A different view of the 'Plan of Campaign' – a Unionist poster condemning the violent methods of the Land League

The murder of a landlord by Land-League assassins during the Land war
of 1879-82

Violence meets violence - an eviction for non-payment of rent in 1880

THE LAND WAR!

NO RENT!

NO LANDLORDS GRASSLAND

Tenant Farmers, now is the time. Now is the hour.
You ~~ y~d false to the first call made upon you.
REDEEM YOUR CHARACTER NOW.

NO RENT

UNTIL THE SUSPECTS ARE RELEASED.

The man who pays Rent (whether an abatement
is offered or not) while PARNELL, DILLON &c.,
are in Jail, will be looked upon as a Traitor to his
Country and a disgrace to his class.

No RENT, No Compromise, No Landlords' Grassland,
Under any circumstances.

Avoid the Police, and listen not to spying and delu-
ding Bailiffs.

NO RENT ! LET THE LANDTHIEVES DO THEIR WORST !

THE LAND FOR THE PEOPLE!

**A Land League poster of 1881**

**In 1881 in an effort to contain the mounting violence, Gladstone's government ordered Parnell to be detained in Dublin's Kilmainhaim Gaol. He was later released on the promise that he would use his influence to limit the violence**

# JUSTICE TO IRELAND!

BRITANNIA (*to* HIBERNIA). "YOU'VE TROUBLES ENOUGH, MY POOR SISTER, WITHOUT *STARVATION*. *THAT* I CAN, AND *WILL*, HELP."

**A *Punch* cartoon attempts to suggest that Britain's concern for conditions in Ireland is genuinely humanitarian**

## "A DANIEL COME TO JUDGMENT!"

SHADE OF O'CONNELL. "EVERY MAN WHO IS GUILTY OF THE SLIGHTEST BREACH OF THE LAW IS AN ENEMY TO IRELAND. *NO POLITICAL REFORM IS WORTH THE SHEDDING OF ONE DROP OF BLOOD.*" (*See* JUSTIN M'CARTHY'S *History.*)

**Punch invokes the spirit of O'Connell to suggest that he would have opposed the violence of the extreme nationalists in Ireland**

The situation in Ireland took a dramatic turn in 1882 when Gladstone's nephew, Lord Frederick Cavendish, the newly-appointed Chief Secretary for Ireland, was murdered along with the Under Secretary, Thomas Burke, in Phoenix Park Dublin. The assassins were the 'Invincibles', an off-shoot of the Irish Republican Brotherhood

Gladstone weighs the alternatives in 1886. He intended his Home Rule
Bill to achieve what coercion alone could not - 'an Irish content'

An Ulster-Unionist postcard of 1912, appealing to Britain not to break the historic and economic links that bind Ulster and the United Kingdom

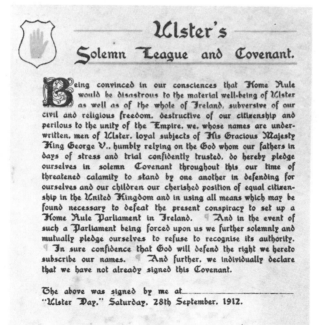

Claims vary, but it is likely that over 250,000 Unionists signed this Covenant

## THE FIGHT FOR THE BANNER.

JOHN BULL. "THIS TIRES ME. WHY CAN'T YOU CARRY IT BETWEEN YOU? NEITHER OF YOU CAN CARRY IT ALONE."

**Britain, represented by John Bull, calls on Edward Carson, the Ulster Unionist leader, and John Redmond, the Irish Nationalist leader, to work together for peace**

A 1914 Ulster-Unionist postcard, showing Captain Craig, a loyalist hero, throttling Asquith and trampling on Redmond

A 1914 Nationalist poster, calling on Irish patriots to enlist in the Irish National Volunteers, a counter army to the Ulster Defence Volunteers

**A 1914 government recruiting poster, calling on Irishmen to fight for Britain**

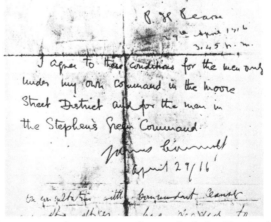

**The surrender document that meant the end of the Easter Rising in 1916**

**One of the series of executions of the leaders of the Easter Rising. It was such reprisals that turned the rebels, who had been previously highly unpopular with the bulk of the Irish people, into heroes**

*LEAFLET No. 12.]*      *[SECOND SERIES.*

# Tyrants of the National League

## BOYCOTTING THE BABE UNBORN.

A SMALL landed Proprietor and Farmer, of County Wexford, examined before LORD COWPER'S Commission on his experience in resisting Boycotting, gave the following example :—

JAMES BURKE, a black sheep in the eyes of the National League, for having paid his rent, was consequently Boycotted.

• • • • Burke's child became ill of bowel complaint. The coarse yellow meal produced this disease. He went to a neighbouring country shop to get white bread or white flour—I forget which—for his sick child, and he was refused it. They would not give it to him. I was away at the time. Of course, when my wife heard it, she immediately sent everything they wanted. But that sick child was refused what was necessary for its health on account of Burke's crime, of taking an evicted farm.

Last Summer a younger child still—one lately born—the local midwife refused to attend the wife in her confinement ; and she was delivered by the aid of an old woman, who was the only person to do anything for him. The child that was lately born became ill and died. Not a person came to the wake. There was no wake at all. Now every Irish person knows what that means ; for every person in the country makes it a religion almost, to go to the wake of a neighbour. Not a person came. Burke told me himself that men were posted on the fences to hinder any person from coming to the funeral. That is a very pregnant thing in Ireland. And Burke had to carry his child to the Roman Catholic churchyard on his own cart. He could get no person to dig the grave for him, and he had to dig the grave himself for his own child.

**Irish Loyal and Patriotic Union leaflet (1887)**

63

# 6

## FENIANISM

## AND THE LAND LEAGUE

With hindsight, it may be argued that the Great Famine had a beneficial side; the drop in population that resulted from mass emigration helped to create a better balance between food resources and need. Such a detached view did not prevail at the time. The bitterness of those Irish who escaped the famine, whether as survivors or emigrants, found its most violent form in Fenianism. This movement, which took its name from `Fianna', the warriors of Irish legend, came into being in 1858 simultaneously in Dublin and New York. It pledged itself to drive the English out of Ireland by force. The struggle was carried to the mainland in the 1860s, with Fenian outrages involving the deaths of civilians and policemen in Manchester and London. Gladstone, during his first Liberal administration, 1868-74, set himself the task of pacifying Ireland, but despite his good intentions his reforms relating to land, religion and education, did little to lessen the bitterness. The number of evictions and retaliatory outrages mounted. [A – B]

Fenianism was not the only Irish reaction. Equally significant was the Land League. Founded in 1879, this organisation aimed at breaking the grip of the landlords as a step towards independence for Ireland. [C – E] Modern scholars emphasise that whatever their social privileges may have been, and however much they were disliked as exploiters by their tenants, the landlords were themselves suffering from economic decline. Their income from rents rarely met overheads [F].

The Land League's first president was Charles Stewart Parnell, who was to become as outstanding a spokesman of Irish hopes as O'Connell had been earlier in the century. Parnell, a Protestant landowner, was driven by a deep and abiding detestation of the British. He advocated a two-fold strategy: in Ireland, a campaign of rent-strikes against landlords, at Westminster, a programme of obstruction by the Irish MPs of govern-ment and parliamentary business. That a movement which was anti-landlord and supported by Catholics should have been led by someone who was both a landlord and a Protestant suggests the complexities and cross-currents that made up Irish nationalism.

Although the League had a constitutional front, it adopted radical, activist, methods from the beginning. The violent period that followed became known as the `land war'. [G – I] Gladstone persisted in his efforts to solve the outstanding problems, but whatever the merits of his intended reforms, they were seen as concessions wrung from an unwilling English administration. [K] Gladstone's government tried both coercion and conciliation. Parnell, who had been imprisoned on suspicion of sedition was released in return for promising to use his influence to lessen the violence in Ireland. [L – N]

The Land League did not achieve its immediate objectives, but it did arouse national consciousness to new heights. Moreover, it could be argued that the Irish land question was effectively solved by Wyndham's Act in 1903. This measure, introduced by a Conservative government, granted substantial proprietorship to former tenants and compensated the dispossessed landlords. However, by that time the land issue was no longer the outstanding question affecting Anglo-Irish relations. It had been superseded by the Home Rule movement and the drive towards Irish independence.

## A  Evictions meet with resistance

On arriving at Ballyvara, I found about 400 men and about 100 boys and women assembled in the fields at each side of the road and on the hills adjoining. The former, many of whom I believe were strangers, were armed with spade, pitchforks and bludgeons, and on my approaching them with the police force alone, they flourished their weapons, set up a shout of defiance, and moved somewhat towards us, with a decided appearance of hostile intention. I immediately advanced, and having read the proclamation prescribed by the Riot Act, I rode into the crowd and warned them in the most earnest manner of the fatal consequences that must have attended any violence on their part. Some of them received my admonition with respectful attention ... but others of them were so violent in their demeanour that I was obliged to order three of them into custody, and but for the steadiness of the police and the proximity of the military at the moment, there is no room to doubt that a conflict must have ensued ... I did not see any fire-arms with them, but have reason to know that some of them had pistols concealed on their persons, and I believe that many of them had come to the meeting from distant parts of the country.

from an account by an English official (1846)

## B  The making of a Fenian

Almost my first-remembered experience of my own life and of the existence of landlordism was our eviction in 1852, when I was about five years of age. That eviction and the privations of the preceding famine years, the story of the starving peasantry of Mayo, of the deaths from hunger and the coffinless graves on the roadside - everywhere a hole could be dug for the slaves who died because of 'God's providence' - all this was the political food seasoned with a mother's tears over unmerited sorrows and sufferings which had fed my mind in another land, a teaching which lost none of its force or directness by being imparted in the Gaelic tongue, which was almost always spoken in our Lancashire home. My first knowledge and impressions of landlordism were got in that school, with an assistant monitor of a father who had been the head of some agrarian secret society in Mayo in 1837, and who had to fly to England in that year to escape a threatened prosecution.

from *The Fall of Feudalism in Ireland* by Michael Davitt (1904)

### C  Tenant self-protection – the Resolutions of the Tenant-right Conference of 1850

1 That a fair valuation of rent between landlord and tenant in Ireland is indispensable.

2 That the tenant shall not be disturbed in his possession so long as he pays the rent fixed by the proposed law.

3 That the tenant shall have a right to sell his interest, with all its incidents, at the highest market value.

4 That where the rent has been fixed by valuation, no rent beyond the valued rent shall be recoverable by any process of law.

5 That cases of minors and other exceptional cases be considered hereafter in any measure to be introduced into parliament.

from *The Freeman's Journal* (August 1850)

### D The landlords experience economic difficulties

Agricultural output, labour costs and rents 1850-86. These curves show fluctuations at current prices from a base of 100 in 1850, when output was £35 million, labour costs £11.5 million and rents £10.4 million.

from W.E.Vaughan, *Landlords and Tenants in Ireland 1848-1904*

**E   A Children's Land League and a Ladies Land League were set up in 1881**

A is the army that covers the ground;
B is the buckshot we're getting all round;
C is the crowbar of cruellest fame;
D is our Davitt, a right glorious name;
E is the English who've robbed us of bread;
F is the famine they've left us instead;
G is for Gladstone, whose life is a lie;
H is the harvest we'll hold or we'll die;
I is the inspector, who when drunk is bold;
J is the jarvey, who'll not drive him for gold;
K is Kilmainham, where our true men abide;
L is the Land League, our hope and our pride;
M is the Magistrate, who makes black of our white;
N is no rent, which will make our wrongs right;
O is Old Ireland, that yet shall be free'd;
P is the Peelers, who sold her for greed;
Q is the Queen, whose use is not known;
R is the Rifles, who keep up her throne;
S is the sheriff, with woe in his train;
T is the toil that others may gain;
U is the Union that works bitter harm;
V is the villain that grabs up the farm;
W is the warrant for death or for chains;
X is the 'Express', all lies and no brains;
Y is 'Young Ireland' spreading the light;
Z is the zeal that will win the great fight.

the alphabet of the Children's Land League (1881)

**F   The Land League expresses its radical aims, 1879**

The land of Ireland belongs to the people of Ireland, to be held and cultivated for the sustenance of those whom God declared to be inhabitants thereof. Land being created to supply mankind with the necessities of existence, those who cultivate it to that end have a higher claim to its absolute possession than those who make it an article of barter, to be used or disposed of for profit or pleasure. The end for which the land of a country is created requires an equitable distribution of the same among the people who live upon the fruits of their labour in its cultivation.

from *the Declaration of Principles* (1879)

### G Parnell advocates the tactic of 'boycotting'
Now, what are you to do to a tenant who bids for a farm from which another tenant has been evicted? (Several voices: 'Shoot him'.) I think I heard somebody say shoot him (cheers). I wish to point out to you a very much better way – a more Christian and charitable way, which will give the lost man an opportunity of repenting (laughter, and hear, hear). When a man takes a farm from which another has been evicted you must shun him on the roadside when you meet him – you must shun him in the streets of the town – you must shun him in the shop - you must shun him in the fair-green and in the market place, and even in the place of worship, by leaving him alone, by putting him into a moral Coventry, by isolating him from the rest of his country as if he were the leper of old – you must show him your detestation of the crime he has committed. If you do this, you may depend on it there will be no man so full of avarice – so lost to shame – as to dare the public opinion of all the right-thinking men in the county and transgress your unwritten code of laws.

from a speech by Parnell in County Clare (1880)

### H A French visitor describes the effects of boycotting
On the dusty road before us slowly walking five cows in rather an emaciated condition. Those beasts strike me by an odd appearance which I am unable to make out at first. When I am close to them I see what it is; *they have not tails.* The absence of that ornament gives the poor animals  the awkwardest and most absurd look.
　　I turn to my guide who is laughing in his sleeve.
　　"Look at their master!", he whispers in a low voice.
　　"Well?"
　　"The cows have no tails, and the man has no ears."
It is true. The unlucky wretch vainly endeavoured to hide his head, as round as a cheese, under the brim of his battered old hat; he did not succeed in hiding his deformity.
　　"By Jove! who arranged you in this guise, you and your cows?", I
　　said to the poor devil, stopping before him.
He made a few grimaces before explaining; but the offer of a cigar, that rarely misses its effect, at last unloosed his tongue. He then told me that the Moonlighters had come with a razor to cut his ears, a week after having cut the tails of his cows as a warning.
　　"And what could have been the motive of such cowardly, barbarous
　　mutilation?"
He had accepted work on a *boycotted* farm, though the League had expressly forbidden it; in other words he was what the Irish call a 'land-grabber'.
　　"Where are you going with your cows?"

"To sell them at Listowel, if I may, which is not certain."
"Why is it not certain? Because they are unprovided with a tail? At
the worst that would only prevent them from being made into ox-tail
soup", I say, trying to enliven the conversation by a little joke.
"That's not it," answers the man. "But the interdict applies to the sale
of the cows as well as to having any intercourse with me. I am
forbidden to buy anything, and anyone speaking to me is fined two
shillings."
He seemed to think this perfectly natural and even just.

from *Ireland's Disease: the English in Ireland* by Paschal Grousset (1888)

**I  The number of evictions and outrages illustrate the scale of the
disturbances**

|      | Families evicted | Agrarian outrages |
| ---- | ---------------- | ----------------- |
| 1878 | 980              | 301               |
| 1879 | 1,238            | 863               |
| 1880 | 2,110            | 2,585             |
| 1881 | 3,415            | 4,439             |
| 1882 | 5,201            | 3,433             |
| 1883 | 3,643            | 870               |
| 1884 | 4,188            | 762               |
| 1885 | 3,127            | 944               |
| 1886 | 3,781            | 1,056             |
| 1887 | 3,869            | 883               |
| 1888 | 1,609            | 660               |

**J  The effect of the 'Land War' in Ireland**
The state of the country is undoubtedly most serious. Nor do the
number of outrages by any means represent the [gravity of the
situation], and for this reason: that in many places ... those who would
profit [by outrages] are complete masters of the situation, and their
temptation, therefore, is removed. Nobody dares to evict. Tenants of
evicted farms, even those who have been in possession for more than
a year, are daily giving them up. Eighty persons are under police
protection. We cannot yet say for certain how far the autumn rents
will be paid, but it appears already that in many places tenants have
refused to pay more than government valuation. Landlords will not
agree to this, they will evict, and then a great increase of outrages
may be expected. It will then be too late to give us extra powers. If
they are to be conferred, the decision must be come to at once.

from a description by Earl Cowper, Lord Lieutenant of Ireland (1881)

**K  In 1881 Gladstone tries again to give security to Irish tenants with his `Three F's' Land Act**
On the morning that this Bill passes every landlord and tenant will be subject to certain new provisions of the law of great importance. In the first place, an increase of rent will be restrained by certain rules. In the second place, the compensation for disturbance will be regulated according to different rates. And in the third place – more important probably than any – the right to sell the tenant's interest will be universally established. These are some of the means outside the Court which we propose; but there will also remain to the tenant the full power of going to the Court to fix a judicial rent, which may be followed by judicial tenant right. The judicial rent will entail a statutory term of 15 years ... Evictions will hereafter, we trust, be only for default.

from Gladstone's speech in the Commons (April 1881)

**L  Even when gaoled,  the leaders of the Land League still continue to organise. They issue a 'No-Rent Manifesto'**
Fellow-countrymen! – The hour to try your souls and to redeem your pledges has arrived. The executive of the National Land League, forced to abandon the policy of testing the land act, feels bound to advise the tenant-farmers of Ireland from this day forth to pay no rents under any circumstances to their landlords until the government relinquishes the existing system of terrorism and restores the constitutional rights of the people. Do not be daunted by the removal of your leaders ... Do not be wheedled into compromise of any sort by the threat of eviction. If you only act together in the spirit to which, within the last two years, you have countless times solemnly pledged your vows, they can no more evict a whole nation than they can imprison them.

Our exiled brothers in America may be relied upon to contribute, if necessary, as many millions of money as they have contributed thousands to starve out landlordism and bring English tyranny to its knees. No power on earth except faintheartedness on your own part can defeat you. Landlordism is already staggering under the blows which you have dealt it amid the applause of the world ... One more heroic effort to destroy landlordism at the very source and fount of its existence, and the system which was and is the curse of your race and of your existence will have disappeared forever ... No power of legalized violence can extort one penny from your purses against your will. If you are evicted, you shall not suffer; the landlord who evicts will be a ruined pauper, and the government which supports him with its bayonets will learn in a single winter how powerless is armed force against the will of a united, determined, and self-reliant nation.

Signed CHARLES S. PARNELL, President, Kilmainham Jail;
MICHAEL DAVITT, Hon. Sec. Portland Prison;
THOMAS BRENNAN, Hon Sec. Kilmainham Jail; JOHN DILLON, Head
Organizer, Kilmainham Jail; THOMAS SEXTON, Head Organizer,
Kilmainham Jail; PATRICK EGAN, Treasurer, Paris, 1881

### M Government coercion fails to control the Land League

The suspension of the Habeas Corpus Act had been successful in the
case of the Fenians; we supposed it would be successful in the case
of the Land League. That was the mistake. The League was a bigger
organisation. It extended all over the country. The arrest of the leaders
did not affect it: the local branches were too well organised. For every
man who was arrested there was another ready to take his place. Our
information was wrong. The conspiracy was more widespread and
more deeply rooted than we were led to suppose. It was not a case
for the suspension of the Habeas Corpus Act.

I admit the policy was a failure, or, at least, not as successful as
we anticipated it would be. But under the circumstances, in face of the
representations of the Irish government, it was impossible to avoid
trying it. Remember, too, that if we had not passed a Coercion Act we
could not have got a good Land Bill through. That was a consideration
which weighed much with me, and I think with all of us.

from a speech by John Bright (1881)

### N The government try unofficial negotiation – `The Kilmainham Treaty'

The cabinet are of opinion that the time has now arrived when with a
view to the interests of law and order in Ireland, the three Members of
Parliament who have been imprisoned on suspicion since last
October, should be immediately released; and that the list of suspects
should be examined with a view to the release of all persons not
believed to be associated with crimes. They propose at once to
announce to Parliament their intention to propose, as soon as
necessary business will permit, a bill to strengthen the ordinary law in
Ireland for the security of life and property, while reserving their
discretion with regard to the Life and Property Protection Act (of 1881)
which however, they do not at present think it will be possible to
renew, if a favourable state of affairs shall prevail in Ireland.

from Gladstone's cabinet memorandum (May 1882)

# Questions

1 Of what value are sources A and B to the historian concerned with analysing the roots of Fenianism? **(7 marks)**

2 In what ways do sources C and D represent a conflict of interests between landlord and tenants? **(7 marks)**

3 How far do sources E-I support the contention that the Land League was moderate in its aims but radical in its methods? **(8 marks)**

4 Using the evidence in sources J and K, and your own knowledge, explain why Gladstone's Land Act of 1881 failed to satisfy the Irish tenantry. **(9 marks)**

5 To what extent do sources M and N indicate that the policy advocated by the Land League in Source L had proved successful? **(9 marks)**

# 7 HOME RULE

Parnell's essential aim throughout the Land League agitation was to create a strong parliamentary base among the Irish MPs from which he could agitate for independence. He declared in 1880 that he would not be content 'until we have destroyed the last link which keeps Ireland bound to England'. In effect, Parnell took over the Home Rule movement which under Isaac Butt had been essentially moderate and constitutional, and turned it into an aggressive, obstructive, lobby that dominated the proceedings of Parliament throughout the 1880s. [A – C and G]

Parnell was willing to support either of the two English parties; his only concern was to advance the Irish cause. [D – E] He appreciated that not all English supporters of Home Rule saw it in terms of complete Irish independence, but he was willing to advance in stages if necessary. Parnell's greatest success appeared to come in 1886 when Gladstone, having tried 'to give justice to Ireland' with a series of reforms during his two periods of government, 1868-74 and 1880-86, concluded that the only way an 'Irish contentment' could be achieved was by the granting of Home Rule. [F and H] At the cost of splitting his own party, Gladstone introduced his first Home Rule Bill in 1886, only for it to be defeated on its second reading in the Commons. [I – K]

The subsequent resignation of the Liberal government ushered in two decades of Conservative political domination. That the Conservatives were now identified as Unionists was further indication of the influence the Irish question had in shaping English politics. Arthur Balfour, Irish Chief Secretary (1887-91) and Prime Minister (1902-5) expressed the essential approach of the Conservative Party during their 20 years of government through his policy of 'killing Home Rule by kindness', a mixture of firmness and reform, of which Wyndham's Act was the major example (see page 65).

Gladstone's defeat in 1886 did not weaken his personal commitment to the Irish question. His hope was that with the support of Parnell's group of MPs, who held the parliamentary balance between the Liberals and the Conservatives, he would still be able to achieve Home Rule. What destroyed the chance of this occurring was the break up of the Irish Nationalist Party in 1890, following Parnell's involvement in a divorce scandal. Parnell had gained greatly from his triumph over *The Times's* attempts to discredit him, but he was unable to hold his party together once his adulterous affair with Mrs O'Shea, the wife of a Nationalist MP, became public knowledge. [L – N] Parnell's death in 1891 and the crushing defeat of Gladstone's second Home Rule Bill by the Unionist-dominated House of Lords in 1893, [O] marked the end, for the time being, of militant nationalism. What took its place was a non-political movement which emphasised the need for Ireland to rediscover its cultural roots and participate in a Gaelic revival. [P – Q]

## A  Isaac Butt, the founder of the Home Rule Association in 1870, defines the moderate, federal aim, of the movement

To obtain for our country the right and privilege of managing our own affairs by a parliament assembled in Ireland, composed of Her Majesty, the Sovereign, and her successors, and the Lords and Commons of Ireland. To secure for that parliament  the right of legislating for and regarding all matters relating to the internal affairs of Ireland.

from *Irish Federalism* by Isaac Butt (1875)

## B  Butt explains his strategy

To make an assault all along the whole line of English misgovernment, and to bring forward every grievance of Ireland, and to press the English House of Commons  for their redress ... I believed, and believe still, that if once we got liberal-minded Englishmen fairly to consider how they would redress the grievance of Irish misgovernment,  they would come in the end to the conclusion that they had but one way of giving us good government, and that was by allowing us to govern ourselves.

from a speech by Butt (1877)

## C  Parnell finds Butt's approach unacceptably tame and unrealistic

Now I gladly agree with Mr Butt that it is very possible, and very probable, that he would be able to persuade a fair-minded Englishman in the direction that he has indicated; but I still do not think that the House of Commons is mainly composed of fair-minded Englishmen. If we had to deal with men who were capable of listening to fair arguments  there would be every hope of success for the policy of Mr Butt as carried out in past sessions; but we are dealing with political parties who really consider  the interests of their political organisations as paramount, beyond every other consideration.

from a speech by Parnell (1877)

## D  Early recognition of Parnell's ability to unite the varying elements among the Irish nationalists

I think he [Parnell] *ought to be supported.* He has the idea I held at the starting of the Home Rule organisation – that is the creation of a political link between the conservative and radical nationalists ... The effect of Parnell's attitude has been simply tremendous and if he were supported by 20 or 30 instead of seven he could render really important services. He has many of the qualities of leadership – and time will give him more. He is cool – extremely so and resolute. With the right kind of support behind him and a band of *real* nationalists in the House of Commons he would so remould Irish public opinion as to clear away many of the stumbling blocks in the way of progressive action.

from James O'Kelly to John Devoy (August 1877)

**E   An Irish Nationalist MP describes his leader's aims and strategy**
[Parnell] had made up his mind to use the House of Commons as the platform of Irish agitation, and to unite Home Rule and Land Reform as inseparable elements in the new campaign. His policy was to insist on a full hearing for those great Irish questions in the House of Commons, and, furthermore – and herein lay the great secret of his success – to insist that if the House of Commons would not listen to the story of Irish grievances, it should do no business at all. This was the whole purpose of obstruction as Mr Parnell meant it and planned it. He was confident that if we but got a fair hearing we should make good the justice of our national claims, and his policy was to say to the House of Commons, 'If you will not listen to us, then neither shall you listen to any one else'.

from *The Story of Gladstone's Life* by Justin McCarthy (1898)

**F   Gladstone's thoughts begin to turn towards a political settlement**
About local government for Ireland, the ideas which more and more establish themselves in my mind are such as these.

1 Until we have seriously responsible bodies to deal with us in Ireland, every plan we frame comes to Irishmen, say what we may, as an English plan. As such it is probably condemned. At best it is a one-sided bargain, which binds us, not them ...

4 In truth I should say, that for the Ireland of today, the first question is the rectification of the relations between landlord and tenant ..., the next is to relieve Great Britain from the enormous weight of the government of Ireland unaided by the people, and from the hopeless contradiction in which we stand while we give a parliamentary representation, hardly effective for anything but mischief without the local institutions of self-government which it presupposes, and on which alone it can have a sound and healthy basis.

from Gladstone to W.E.Forster (April 1882)

75

**G While prepared to bargain with both Conservatives and Liberals, Parnell leaves his supporters in little doubt as to his objective**
I come back to the great question of national self-government for Ireland. I do not know how this great question will be eventually settled ... We cannot ask for less than restitution of Grattan's parliament [loud cheers], with its important privileges and wide and far-reaching constitution. We cannot under the British constitution ask for more than the restitution of Grattan's parliament, but no man has the right to fix the boundary to the march of nation. No man has the right to say to his country, 'Thus far shalt thou go and no further', and we have never attempted to fix the *ne plus ultra* to the progress of Ireland's nationhood, and we never shall.

from a speech of Parnell's in Cork (January 1885)

**H His conversion to Home Rule having been revealed in 1885, Gladstone defines his understanding of it to Hartington, the leader of the Whigs**
The conditions of an admissible plan are:
    1 Union of the Empire and due supremacy of parliament.
    2 Protection for the minority – a difficult matter ...
    3 Fair allocation of imperial charges ...
    4 A statutory basis seems to me better and safer than the revival of Grattan's parliament ...
    6 As to intentions, I am determined to have none at present, to leave space to the government – I should wish to encourage them if I properly could – above all, on no account to say or do anything which would enable the nationalists to establish rival biddings between us.

from Gladstone to Lord Hartington (December 1885)

**I Gladstone appreciates the consequences for his Party if he proceeds with Home Rule**
Hartington writes to me a letter indicating ... his determination 'to maintain the legislative union', that is to proclaim a policy (so I understand the phrase) of absolute resistance without examination to the demand made by Ireland through five-sixths of her members. This is to play the tory game with a vengeance. They are now most rashly, not to say more, working the Irish question to split the Liberal Party. It seems to me that if a gratuitous declaration of this kind is made, it must produce an explosion; and that in a week's time Hartington will have to consider whether he will lead the Liberal Party himself, or leave it to chaos. He will make my position impossible.

from Gladstone to Lord Granville (January 1886)

**J  Joseph Chamberlain, leader of the radical Liberals, resigns claiming that Home Rule undermines the integrity of the United Kingdom**
This new programme of Mr Parnell's involves a greater extension than anything we have hitherto known or understood by Home Rule; the powers he claims for his support in Parliament are altogether beyond anything which exists in the case of the State Legislatures of the American Union, which has hitherto been the type and model of Irish demands, and if this claim were conceded we might as well for ever abandon all hope of maintaining a United Kingdom. We should establish within 30 miles of our shores a new foreign country animated from the outset with unfriendly intentions towards ourselves. Such a policy as that, I firmly believe, would be disastrous and ruinous to Ireland herself. It would be dangerous to the security of this country, and under these circumstances I hold that we are bound to take every step in our power to avert so great a calamity.

from Chamberlain's speech at Warrington (September 1885)

**K  Gladstone introduces the first Home Rule Bill, 1886**
What are the results that have been produced [by the Act of Union]? This result above all – and now I come to what I consider to be the basis of the whole mischief – that rightly or wrongly, yet in point of fact, law is discredited in Ireland, and discredited in Ireland upon this ground especially – that it comes to the people of that country with a foreign aspect, and in a foreign garb ...
  I ask you to show to Europe and to America that we, too, can face political problems which America 20 years ago faced, and which many countries in Europe have been called upon to face, and have not feared to deal with. I ask that in our own case we should practise, with firm and fearless hand, what we have so often preached – that the concession of local self-government is not the way to sap or impair, but the way to strengthen and consolidate unity. I ask that we should apply to Ireland that happy experience which we gained in England and in Scotland ... that the best and surest foundation we can find to build upon is the foundation afforded by the affections, the convictions, and the will of the nation; and it is thus, by the decree of the Almighty, that we may be enabled to secure at once the social peace, the fame, the power and the permanence of the Empire.

from Gladstone's speech in the Commons (April 1886)

**L  Arthur Balfour defines the Conservative policy of 'killing Home Rule by kindness'**
I shall be as relentless as Cromwell in enforcing obedience to the law, but, at the same time, I shall be as radical as any reformer in

77

redressing grievances. It is on the twofold aspect of my policy that I rely for success. Hitherto English governments have either been all for repression or all for reform. I am for both: repression as stern as Cromwell; reform as thorough as Mr Parnell or anyone else can desire.

from a letter of Balfour's (1887)

## M The forged letter that appeared in 'Parnellism and Crime'

15/2/82

Dear Sir,

    I am not surprised at your friend's anger, but he and you should know that to denounce the murders was the only course open to us. To do that promptly was plainly our best policy.

    But you can tell him and all the others concerned that though I regret the accident of Lord F. Cavendish's death I cannot refuse to admit that Burke got no more than his deserts.

    You are at liberty to show him this, and others whom you can trust also, but let not my address be known. He can write to the House of Commons.

    Yours very truly,

    Chas.S. Parnell

from *The Times* (April 1887)

## N Following the revelation of Parnell's involvement in the O'Shea divorce case, Gladstone regrets that he can no longer support the Irish leader

I thought it necessary ... to acquaint Mr McCarthy with the conclusion at which, after using all the means of observation and reflection in my power, I had myself arrived. It was that notwithstanding the splendid services rendered by Mr Parnell to his country, his continuance at the present moment in the leadership would be productive of consequences disastrous in the highest degree to the cause of Ireland. I think I may be warranted in asking you so far to expand the conclusion I have given above, as to add that the continuance I speak of would not only place many hearty and effective friends of the Irish cause in a position of great embarrassment, but would render my retention of the leadership of the Liberal Party, based as it has been mainly upon the prosecution of the Irish cause, almost a nullity. This explanation of my views I begged Mr McCarthy to regard as confidential, and not intended for his colleagues generally, if he found that Mr Parnell contemplated spontaneous action; but I also begged that he would make known to the Irish Party, at their meeting tomorrow afternoon, that such was my conclusion, if he should find that Mr Parnell had not in contemplation any step of the nature indicated.

from Gladstone to John Morley (24 November 1890)

**O  Faced with the Liberal Party's abandonment of Parnell, his own Irish Nationalist Party begin to turn bitterly against him**
Mr Parnell for the first time for five years of struggle and suffering and fierce war against the oppressors of Ireland has mounted an Irish platform ... He now comes amongst us to bewilder, to confuse, to divide ... The silence of the Divorce Court is broken with 'I could and I would'. He hints that he has his answer. If he has, let him out with it. If he has, and refuses to speak, we tell him that he is doubling his treason to Ireland, that he is preferring a base desire to the fortunes of his country ... Mr Parnell knows that in talking this way he is talking braggart rot. We are not going into a hopeless rebellion in Ireland for the privilege of retaining the co-respondent of a divorce case as the leader of our nation.

from an editorial in *The Nation* (December 1890)

**P  Gladstone's second Home Rule Bill was manoeuvred through the Commons in 1893 but rejected by the Lords**
We are compelled to accompany that acceptance [of the Bill's defeat] with the sorrowful declaration that the differences, not of a temporary or casual nature merely, but differences of conviction, differences of prepossession, differences of mental habit, and differences of fundamental tendency, between the House of Lords and the House of Commons, appear to have reached a development in the present year such as to create a state of things of which we are compelled to say that, in our judgment, it cannot continue. Sir, I do not wish to use hard words, which are easily employed and as easily retorted – it is a game that two can play at – but without using hard words, without presuming to judge of motives, without desiring or venturing to allege imputations, I have felt it a duty to state what appeared to me to be indisputable facts. The issue which is raised between a deliberative assembly, elected by the votes of more than six million people, and a deliberative assembly occupied by many men of virtue, by many men of talent, of course with considerable diversities and varieties, is a controversy which, when once raised, must go forward to an issue.

from Gladstone's speech in the Commons (March 1894)

**Q Failure to achieve Home Rule redirects nationalist thoughts towards reasserting an Irish cultural identity**
One of the most painful and at the same time, one of the most frequently recurring reflections that, as an Irishman, I am compelled to make is that we are daily importing from England her fashions, her accents, her vicious literature, her music, her dances, and her manifold mannerisms, her games also and her pastimes, to the utter discredit of our own great national sports.

Indeed, if we continue travelling for the next score years in the same direction that we have been going in for some time past, condemning the sports that were practised by our forefathers, effacing our national features as though we were ashamed of them, and putting on, with England's stuffs and broadcloths her master habits, and such other effeminate follies as she may recommend, we had better at once, and publicly, abjure our nationality.

from Archbishop Croke, Patron of the Gaelic Athletic Association (1884)

**R The Gaelic League**
The Gaelic League has the best possible reason for believing that if Ireland is to become a really cultured country, and an artistic country, she must cease to imitate, and must take up the thread of her own past, and develop from within upon native lines. The moment Ireland broke with her own Gaelic past (and that is only a few score years ago), she fell away hopelessly from all intellectual and artistic effort. She lost her musical instruments, she lost her music, she lost her games, she lost her language, she lost her intellectuality ... We believe that the principle of nationality rightly understood, the reverence for antiquity, and the principles of patriotism, have not only a moral but a high economic value as well.

from Douglas Hyde's evidence before the the Royal Commission on University Education (1902)

**S The Marxist trade-union leader James Connolly asserts that the only true path to national revival is by the creation of an Irish workers republic**
The Labour Movement of Ireland must set itself the Re-Conquest of Ireland as its final aim, that the re-conquest involves taking possession of the entire country, all its power of wealth-production and all its natural resources, and organising these on a cooperative basis for the good of all ...

As a cold matter of fact all talk about the 'restoration of our native Parliament' is misreading history. Ireland never had an Irish Parliament – a Parliament representative of the Irish people. The assembly called by the name of an Irish Parliament was in reality as alien to the Irish people as the Council of the Governor-General of India is alien to the Indian people. And some of the laws passed by our so-called native Parliament against the poor Irish peasantry were absolutely revolting in their ferocity and class vindictiveness.

How long will it be until the Socialists realise the folly and inconsistency of preaching to the workers that the emancipation of the working class must be the act of the workers themselves, and yet presenting to those workers the sight of every important position in the party occupied by men not of the working class?

We will get the workers to have trust in their own power to achieve their own emancipation when we demonstrate our belief that there is no task incidental to that end that a worker cannot accomplish; when we train the workers to look inward upon their own class for everything required, to have confidence in the ability of their own class to fill every position in the revolutionary army; when, in short, we of the socialist working class take to heart the full meaning of the term *Sinn Fein,* Ourselves, and apply it to the work of industrial reconstruction, the era of the strutters and poseurs will end and we will realise at last what was meant by Marx when he spoke of the revolt of those who 'have nothing to lose but their chains'.

from Connolly's political writings (1908)

# Questions

1 In the light of sources A-E, describe the essential characteristics that Parnell brought to the the Home Rule movement.　　　**(7 marks)**

2 In what respects do sources F and H differ from source G in their interpretation of Home Rule?　　　**(7 marks)**

3 What insights are offered by sources I-K and P into the reasons for the split in the Liberal ranks over Home Rule?　　　**(10 marks)**

4 Using your own knowledge and the evidence in sources M-O, explain the circumstance in which Parnell came to lose the leadership of the Irish Parliamentary Party in 1890.　　　**(8 marks)**

5 Assess the value of sources Q, R and S to the historian who is studying Irish nationalism.　　　**(8 marks)**

# 8 ULSTER

In trying to solve the Irish question, Gladstone had been acutely aware of the problem of Ulster. [A – B] The Tory radicals, led by Randolph Churchill, played `the orange card' by taking up the unionist cause: `Ulster will fight and Ulster will be right'. [C] In Ulster, a movement to resist Home Rule developed that was as resolute as that of the Irish Nationalists. The Unionists' fear was that if Ireland were to be granted independence this would result in their being subordinated to the Catholic South: `Home Rule means Rome rule'. [D – E] Thus by a curious twist of history Unionists found themselves at the end of the 19th century in the same position as Nationalists at the end of the 18th century - looking to union with Britain as the necessary guarantee of their interests.

In economic terms the Ulster region, particularly Belfast, was the most industrially advanced and prosperous region in Ireland. [F] This made Nationalists determined that the area should remain part of the nation should Ireland ever be granted separation. Clearly the unionist and Nationalist viewpoints were wholly irreconcilable. [G – H] Any attempt to solve the Irish question was now certain to fall foul of the Ulster issue.

The Home Rule story took another dramatic turn in 1911. This was the year of the Parliament Act which ended the House of Lords' veto over Commons legislation. The Act had been occasioned by the rejection by the Conservative-dominated House of Lords of the 1909 People's Budget, but for Unionists it had an ominous bearing on the Irish question. The reduction in the powers of the Lords meant that there was now no constitutional way to prevent the Liberals forcing through Home Rule. Asquith's government, supported by John Redmond 's Irish Nationalist MPs, could carry the Bill through the Commons, knowing that the Lords could no longer prevent it becoming law. This produced a desperate reaction among the Unionists. [I – J] Following Asquith's introduction in 1912 of the third Home Rule Bill, Ulster prepared for violent confrontation.

Edward Carson, the leader of the Protestant Covenanters, claimed that the two general elections of 1910, which had wiped out the Liberals' majority and left them dependent on the Irish Nationalist MPs, had deprived the Liberal government of an electoral mandate for Home Rule. [K] Carson called upon the Unionists to `use all means which may be necessary' to prevent the measure being implemented. By the summer of 1914, what were in effect two armies, the Protestant Ulster

Volunteers and the Nationalist Irish Volunteers, prepared for civil war.
[L – N] That the Ulstermen were by far the better armed of the two sides
did not lessen the Nationalists' willingness to fight.

Still believing that a compromise was possible, Asquith proposed that
the Home Rule terms should not be applied in Ulster for six years. He
had some success. In July 1914, with war against Germany imminent, it
was agreed between the parties that the operation of the Home Rule Bill
would be suspended for the duration of the war. This produced a
temporary easing of the situation, but it was clear the issue was far from
settled.

## A  The Orange Order had earlier shown its fierce resistance to Gladstone's proposals to disestablish the Irish Church

We have – I should rather say we had – a Protestant Constitution. The
guardianship of that Constitution was committed to the king, Lords
and Commons, the rulers of this Protestant kingdom. So long as they
discharged their trust as honest men, there was no necessity to seek
to withdraw it from their charge, but as soon as these guardians
betrayed their trust and commenced, step by step, to assail that
Constitution, break down the most precious bulwarks, and seek to
destroy the Protestant faith, then it became a duty, and an actual
necessity, to take upon ourselves the duty which they neglected to
perform - to do the work that belonged to the government of a
Protestant land, for the Protestant subjects of that land.

from a speech of Brother W.J.Gwyn of the Orange Lodge Belfast (1867)

## B  When introducing the first Home Rule Bill, Gladstone alludes to the intractable problem of Ulster

The strong instincts of the Irish people require, not only that laws
should be good, but that they should proceed from a congenial and
native source, and besides being good laws, they should be their own
laws.

We seek the settlement of that question in the establishment of a
Parliament sitting in Dublin, for the conduct of Irish, as distinct from
Imperial affairs. That is my postulate, from which I set out ... The
essential conditions of any plan are, that the unity of the Empire
must not be placed in jeopardy, and next that there should be
reasonable safeguards for the Protestant minority, especially in the
Province of Ulster.

But, Sir, I cannot allow it to be said, that a Protestant minority in
Ulster, or elsewhere, is to rule the question at large for Ireland, when
five-sixths of its chosen representatives are of one mind in this matter
....

from a speech by Gladstone in the House of Commons (1886)

**C  Randolph Churchill leads the Tory-radical attack upon Home Rule**
I decided some time ago, that if the G.O.M. [Gladstone] went for
Home Rule, the Orange card should be the one to play. Please God it
may turn out the ace of trumps and not the two ...

If political parties and political leaders, not only parliamentary but
local, should be so utterly lost to every feeling and dictate of honour
and courage as to hand over coldly, and for the sake of purchasing a
short and illusory Parliamentary tranquillity, the lives and liberties of
the Loyalists of Ireland to their hereditary and most bitter foes, make
no doubt on this point - Ulster will not be a consenting party: Ulster
at the proper moment will resort to the supreme arbitrament of force;
Ulster will fight, Ulster will be right; Ulster will emerge from the
struggle victorious, because all that Ulster represents to us Britons will
command the sympathy and support of an enormous  section of our
British community.

from letters and speeches of Randolph Churchill  (1886)

**D  Anxious not to lose their dominant position in northern Ireland,
the Protestants assert the merits of the Act of Union**
We but repeat, what is well known to everyone who has bestowed
attention on the subject, that, in every detail which goes to make up
the sum of civilised life, the Irish people are at this moment very far
in advance of the condition of their ancestors at the time of the Union.
They are better housed, better clad, better fed: they receive better
prices for the produce of their farms, and higher wages for their
labour; they have greater liberty and better protection in health,
abundant provision for sickness, and facilities for the education and
advancement in life of their children, such as were undreamt of 80
years ago. No measure has been passed, since the Union, for the
benefit of the English or the Scotch people, in which they have not
shared; and many Acts have been passed specially for their benefit
which have not been extended to Scotland or England. These are facts
which cannot be controverted, and which no one, except hireling
agitators, would attempt to deny or distort.

an address by the 'Irish Loyal and Patriotic Union' to Gladstone (1886)

**E  Supported by Tory-radicals at Westminster, the Orange Order
re-emerges at the time of the Home Rule Bills as the voice of Irish
Protestantism and the defender of the Union**
We solemnly resolve and declare that we express the devoted loyalty
of Ulster Unionists to the Crown and constitution of the United
Kingdom; that we avow our fixed resolve to retain unchanged our
present position as an integral part of the United Kingdom;  that we

declare to the people of Great Britain our conviction that the attempt to set up such an all-Irish Parliament will result in disorder, violence and bloodshed.

from the resolution of the Ulster Convention League (1892)

**F A description of the religious divide in Belfast at the beginning of the 20th century**
Belfast is a great manufacturing town, which in progress and wealth enjoys a foremost place among the centres of population of the United Kingdom. Its population in 1881, according to the census returns, was 208,122, and since that time has probably increased to about 230,000. It has an area of 6,805 acres, and a valuation of £604,537. The town is, in its present proportions, of very recent growth; and the result is that the poorer classes, instead of, as in other cities, occupying tenements in large houses, reside mainly in separate quarters, each of which is almost entirely given up to persons of one particular faith, and the boundaries of which are sharply defined. In the district of West Belfast, the great thoroughfare of the Shankill-road, with the network of streets running into it, and the side streets connecting those lateral branches, is an almost purely Protestant district; and the parties referred to in the evidence as 'the Shankill mob', are a Protestant mob. The great Catholic quarter is due south of the Shankill district, and consists of the thoroughfare known as the Falls-road, and the streets running south of it; and the parties referred to in the testimony before us as the 'Falls-road mob', are therefore a Catholic mob. Due south of the Falls district is Grosvenor-street; almost entirely inhabited by Protestants, so that the Catholic quarter lies between two Protestant districts. The Shankill-road and Falls-road are both largely inhabited by shopkeepers who supply the wants of the population, and whose houses are sometimes large and comfortable. The streets running off these thoroughfares consist of long rows of cottages of artisans and labourers. The great points of danger to the peace of the town are open spaces in the border land between the two quarters; and two of these spaces – the Brickfields and Springfield – will be found to have been the theatres of some of the worst scenes of the riots.
 The great number of working people who dwell in the districts we have described are, at ordinary times, a most peaceable and industrious community. But unfortunately a spirit has grown up amongst these people, which has resulted in that, on three previous occasions within the last 30 years, in 1857, 1864, and 1872, the town was the scene of disturbances and long-continued riots.

from the *Report of the Belfast Riot Commissioners* (1887)

## G  The Orangemen declare their total opposition to Home Rule

We the Orangemen of the Loyal Orange District of Fivemiletown in the Co. of Tyrone hereby declare our steadfast adherence to the principles of civil and religious liberty thereby established in these realms, and our first determination to lay down our lives in their defence rather than allow them to be wrested from us ...

In common with our loyalist fellow subjects in England and Scotland as well as in Ireland we deprecate the insidious and profligate and unpatriotic attempt now being made by a self seeking and reckless old politician [Gladstone] abetted by a motley and heterogeneous rabble of professional agitators to smuggle through the House of Commons, with[out] the necessary full debate of its provisions a measure calculated to uproot the Constitution under which we live and to imperil our lives, our liberties and our worldly substance ... Lastly, we would record our undying allegiance to the Gracious Monarch who has so long and so wisely wielded the sceptre over the Mighty Empire of which Ireland forms an integral part, our ardent attachment to the Constitution of the United Kingdom, and our fixed resolve never to submit to laws enacted by an Irish Parliament of which the members would be the nominees and puppets of the Roman Priesthood.

from the `Orange resolutions' (July 1893)

## H  Doubt is cast on the religious motivation behind sectarianism

[T]here is a cast-iron bigotry – a cruel corroding, unfathomable, ferocious, sectarian rancour ... Orange hostility to Catholicism is largely due to sordid political enmity, or, in other words, to hard cash. Sectarianism is being used for a political end. It is not religious zeal. It is merely inherited spite ... There are Catholics ready to take their lives into their hands on St Patrick's Day who may not have complied with their religious duties for years. There are Orangemen ready to cry `To Hell with the Pope' who have not been inside of a church since their boyhood. They are born to it, brought up to it. It is an inheritance, this blind unreasoning hatred.

from *Rambles in Erin* by William Buffin (1907)

## I  Disturbed by the commitment of the Liberals under Asquith to re-introduce Home Rule, the Unionists issue a 'Manifesto' at the time of the 1910 general elections

One million five hundred thousand of your fellow subjects in Ireland, that is to say, about one-third of the whole population of the country, call for your help at the polls. They are loyally devoted to the Legislative Union between Great Britain and Ireland under which they

have been born and lived. They include, beside many thousands of
scattered Royalists in the West and South of Ireland, the
overwhelming majority of the most progressive and prosperous parts
of Ulster, including the great city of Belfast. They compromise
Episcopalians, Presbyterians, Methodists, and other religious
persuasions including a minority of loyal Roman Catholics. Be assured
that they know from experience the danger under Home Rule of
religious, social and political tyranny from the men who have been the
enemies of Great Britain. We are convinced that the injury caused by
Home Rule to the great industries of the North and other parts of
Ireland would send thousands of workmen to your shores competing
with you for employment and adding to the existing mass of
unemployed ... We are certain that a country within a few miles of
you governed by those who have shown their hostility to Great Britain
may constitute, especially at the present time, a standing menace to
you from a naval and military point of view.

from the `Manifesto to the Electors of Great Britain' (1910)

**J Edward Carson, the leading spokesman for Irish Unionism, sees
the danger for Protestant Ulster that follows from the 1911 Parliament Bill**
We must be prepared, in the event of a Home Rule Bill passing, with
such measures as will carry on for ourselves the government of those
districts of which we have control. We must be prepared ... the
morning Home Rule passes, ourselves to become responsible for the
government of the Protestant province of Ulster.

from a speech by Edward Carson at a Unionist rally in Belfast (1911)

**K The Elections of 1910 throw doubt on the Liberals' mandate for
Home Rule**

| Jan/Feb Election | Votes | seats | % vote |
|---|---|---|---|
| Conservatives | 3,127,887 | 273 | 46.9 |
| Liberals | 2,880,581 | 275 | 43.2 |
| Labour | 505,657 | 40 | 7.6 |
| Irish Nationalists | 124,586 | 82 | 1.9 |
| December Election | | | |
| Conservatives | 2,420,566 | 272 | 46.3 |
| Liberals | 2,295,888 | 272 | 43.9 |
| Labour | 371,772 | 42 | 7.1 |
| Irish Nationalists | 131,375 | 84 | 2.5 |

**L  Over 200,000 Unionists formally commit themselves to resist the introduction of Home Rule**
Being convinced in our consciences  that Home Rule would be disastrous to the material well-being of Ulster as well as of the whole of Ireland, subversive of our civil and religious freedom, destructive of our citizenship and perilous to the unity of the Empire, we, whose names are underwritten, men of Ulster, loyal subjects of His Gracious Majesty, King George V, humbly relying on the God whom our fathers in days of stress and trial confidently trusted, do hereby pledge ourselves in solemn covenant  throughout this our time of threatened calamity to stand by one another in defending for ourselves and our children our cherished position of equal citizenship in the United Kingdom and in using all means which may be found necessary to defeat the present conspiracy to set up a Home Rule Parliament in Ireland. And in the event of such a Parliament being forced upon us we further solemnly and mutually pledge ourselves to refuse to recognise its authority. In sure confidence that God will defend the right we hereto subscribe our names.

from the Solemn League and Covenant (September 1912)

**M  Bonar Law, the Conservative leader, declares his willingness to defy the law in his support of the Ulster Unionists**
In our opposition ... we shall not be guided by the considerations  or bound by the restraints which would influence us in an ordinary constitutional struggle ... They may, perhaps they will, carry their Home Rule Bill through the House of Commons, but what then? I said the other day in the House of Commons and I repeat here that there are things stronger than parliamentary majorities ...

I can imagine no length of resistance to which Ulster can go in which I should not be prepared to support  them, and in which, in my belief, they would not be supported by the overwhelming majority of the British people ...

We regard the government  as a revolutionary committee which has seized by fraud upon despotic power. In our opposition to them ... we shall not be restrained by the bonds, which would influence our action in any ordinary political struggle.

from speeches by Bonar Law  (1912)

**N  Lord Dunleath, one of the organisers, explains how the Ulster Volunteer Force (UVF), an unofficial army of 100,000, came into being in 1913 prepared to fight Home Rule**
We felt that it was the plain duty of those of us who were possessed of influence to take some step, which would convince the government

of the reality of our determination to resist this policy by every means in our power ... We commenced by drilling our Orangemen and our Unionist Clubs, wherever drill instructors could be obtained, and suitable halls and lodges were available. Later on we amalgamated these forces, organised them into companies and battalions, appointed officers and section leaders, and gradually equipped and trained them into a very fairly efficient force of volunteer infantry. Finally we succeeded in providing them with a good supply of arms and ammunition. We can certainly claim that we have succeeded in turning the attention of Englishmen and Scotchmen towards Ulster and its inhabitants; we can also claim that the existence of this large armed force of Volunteers has materially assisted our political leaders.

from Lord Dunleath to Edward Carson (1914)

# Questions

**1** Comment on the significance of the following references:
   **a** 'We have – I should rather say we had – a Protestant Constitution.' (source A, line 1)                    **(4 marks)**
   **b** 'reasonable safeguards for the Protestant minority' (Source B, line 10)                    **(4 marks)**
   **c** 'Ulster will fight, Ulster will be right' (source C, line 11) **(4 marks)**
   **d** 'our fixed resolve to retain unchanged our present position as an integral part of the United Kingdom' (source E, line 3) **(5 marks)**

**2** How far does the description in source F bear out the claims made in source D?                    **(7 marks)**

**3** In the light of your own knowledge and the evidence in sources G-I, judge whether economic or religious concerns had the greater influence on the shaping of Unionist attitudes.                    **(8 marks)**

**4** To what extent does the evidence in source K support the claims made by the Unionists in sources J and M in justification of their willingness to act outside the law in opposing Home Rule? **(8 marks)**

**5** How far does the evidence in sources H-N support the contention that by 1914 Ulster had become an intractable political problem?                    **(10 marks)**

# 9

# THE TROUBLES
# AND THE TREATY

Although weakened by the Parnell scandal in 1890, the Irish Nationalist MPs in the Commons had continued to function as a party. They gained an increase in influence after the election results of 1910, which left Asquith's Liberal government reliant on them for its parliamentary majority. John Redmond, the leader of the Irish MPs, played a major role in the introduction of the third Home Rule Bill in 1912. However, during the same period developments occurred which were as important as the recovery of the Irish party at Westminster. In 1908 a number of nationalist groups in Ireland came together in Ireland under the banner of Sinn Fein. According to its chief spokesman, Arthur Griffith, Sinn Fein's aim was to break both the political and the economic stranglehold Britain held over Ireland. Griffith, who regarded Redmond as being too moderate, opposed the 1912 Home Rule Bill because it did not go far enough towards establishing Ireland's independence.

The division in Irish nationalist opinion became particularly marked following the outbreak of the First World War. Whether Irishmen should fight for Britain became a major question. Redmond believed they should. [A] Griffith and Pearse bitterly opposed such a notion; if the Irish were to fight it should be against Britain. [B – C] In April 1916 this happened. Hoping to profit from Britain's pre-occupation with the war in Europe, a grouping of nationalists and socialists, including James Connolly's Citizen Army and Patrick Pearse's splinter group of Irish Volunteers, seized a number of key buildings in Dublin and declared that the Irish Republic had come into being. [D] Though dramatic, this `Easter Rising' was a small-scale and ill-organised affair; it aroused little support either in Dublin or in Ireland at large and was easily crushed. [E] Nonetheless, it proved a watershed in Anglo-Irish relations. The severity with which the British authorities were held to have treated the defeated rebels kindled rather than dimmed the fires of nationalism. [F – H] The next five years were those of the `Troubles', a period when violence was met with violence, most dramatically in the confrontation between the IRA, the military wing of Sinn Fein, and the government's specially-recruited anti-terrorist squads, known from their distinctive uniform as the Black and Tans. [I – L]

Disturbed by the scale of the `Troubles', which reached a peak in the years 1919-21, Lloyd George became convinced that nothing short of independence would satisfy Irish nationalist demands. He initiated a series of complex discussions with the various Irish parties. The greatest obstacle to a solution was the attitude of the Unionists in Ulster. Eventually, their fears were becalmed sufficiently for them to accept the Irish Treaty of 1921, which set up the Irish Free State, made up of the the 26 counties of the South, with the six predominantly-Protestant counties of Northern Ireland remaining as part of the United Kingdom. The treaty was a flawed document. [M] Its compromises left many in Ireland deeply unhappy, as the bitter civil war that followed in the Free State between pro and anti-treaty factions soon showed. [N − R] Nonetheless, the treaty which became operative in 1922 meant that the troubled phase of Anglo-Irish relations that had begun with the Act of Union had ended.

**A   John Redmond is anxious to prove to the British Government that the Irish Nationalists are as willing as the Unionists to fight for Britain against Germany**
There seems to be a concerted effort on foot to induce the belief in this country that Ireland is declining to bear her fair share of the burden of the war in the matter of recruits, and I think it well, therefore, to bring certain matters under the attention of the government ...

The delay in the formation of the Irish Brigade which was asked for by me in the middle of September [1914], and which was promised by the Prime Minister in his speech in the Mansion House, Dublin, so far back as the 25 September, has had a most injurious and disheartening effect. For many weeks, the Irish people have had paraded before them the fact that Sir Edward Carson and his friends had succeeded in obtaining an Ulster Volunteer Division, officially styled, officered by leading members of the Ulster Volunteer force, and with distinctive Ulster Volunteer badge; and, on the other side, a tacit refusal on the part of the authorities to allow the formation of an Irish Brigade for the South and West ...

In spite of all this, my information is that recruiting is progressing steadily. I have asked for a return to be made by the police of the number of recruits ... This can easily be done, and will show at a glance the number of Nationalists who have enlisted ...

Under these circumstances, I would ask the Prime Minister to give me an interview at the earliest possible moment on these points.

from a Memorandum (November 1914)

**B   Arthur Griffith, the Sinn Fein leader, regards Redmond's attempt to commit Irishmen to the war as a betrayal of the nationalist cause**
Ireland is not at war with Germany. She has no quarrel with any continental power. England is at war with Germany, and Mr Redmond

has offered England the services of the Volunteers to defend Ireland. What has Ireland to defend, and whom has she to defend it against?

Our duty is in no doubt. We are Irish nationalists, and the only duty we can have is to stand for Ireland's interests, irrespective of the interests of England, or Germany, or any other foreign country.

from Arthur Griffith (1914)


**C  A key figure who broke away from Redmond over this issue was the Gaelic poet, Patrick Pearse. He believed that the war offered a great opportunity for a rising of Irish patriots not for but against Britain. His constant theme was the need for sacrifice**
To break the connection with England, the never-failing source of all our political evils, and to assert the independence of his country ... Such is the high and sorrowful destiny of the heroes: to turn their backs to the pleasant paths and their faces to the hard paths, to blind their eyes to the fair things of life ... and to follow only the far, faint call that leads them into the battle or to the harder death at the foot of a gibbet ...

The European War has brought about a crisis which may contain, as yet hidden within it, the moment for which the generations have been waiting. It remains to be seen whether, if that moment reveals itself, we shall have the sight to see and the courage to do; or whether it shall be written of this generation, alone of all the generations of Ireland, that it had none among it who dared to make the ultimate sacrifice ...

Life springs from death; and from the graves of patriot men and women spring living nations. The Defenders of this Realm have worked well in secret and in the open. They think that they have pacified Ireland. They think that they have purchased half of us and intimidated the other half. They think that they have foreseen everything, think that they have provided against everything; but the fools, the fools, the fools! – they have left us our Fenian dead, and while Ireland holds these graves, Ireland unfree shall never be at peace.

from the writings and speeches of Patrick Pearse (1913-16)


**D  In April 1916 the long-awaited nationalist rising that Pearse had prophesied took place**
**Proclamation of the Irish Republic, issued 24 April 1916**
The Provisional Government of the Irish Republic to the People of Ireland.
**Irishmen and Irishwomen:** In the name of God and of the dead generations from which she receives her old tradition of nationhood,

Ireland, through us, summons her children to her flag and strikes for her freedom.

Having organised and trained her manhood through her secret revolutionary organisation, the Irish Republican Brotherhood, and through her open military organisations, the Irish Volunteers, and the Irish Citizen Army, having patiently perfected her discipline, having resolutely waited for the right moment to reveal itself, she now seizes that moment, and, supported by her exiled children in America and by gallant allies in Europe, but relying in the first on her own strength, she strikes in full confidence of victory.

We declare the right of the people of Ireland to the ownership of Ireland, and to the unfettered control of Irish destinies, to be sovereign and indefeasible. The long usurpation of that right by a foreign people and government has not extinguished the right, nor can it ever be extinguished except by the destruction of the Irish people. In every generation the Irish people have asserted their right to national freedom and sovereignty; six times during the past 300 years they have asserted it in arms. Standing on that fundamental right and again asserting it in arms in the face of the world, we hereby proclaim the Irish Republic as a sovereign independent state, and we pledge our lives and the lives of our comrades-in-arms to the cause of its freedom, of its welfare, and of its exaltation among the nations.

Signed on behalf of the Provisional Government,
Thomas J.Clarke, Sean MacDiarmada, Thomas MacDonagh,
P.H.Pearse, Eamon Ceannt, James Connolly, Joseph Plunkett

**E Aware that a successful nationalist rising required a large supply of weapons, Sir Roger Casement had attempted to smuggle German arms into Ireland. He was caught shortly before the Easter Rising and was later tried and shot as a traitor to Britain. In a letter of 1915 he expresses his frustration at the lack of real support among the Irish at home or abroad for armed rebellion**
I want help. I am here alone. I want officers. I want men. I want a fighting fund ... I came here [the USA] for one thing only, to try and help national Ireland and if there is no such thing in existence then the sooner I pay for my illusions the better ... This will be really a test – probably a final one – of the sincerity of Irish nationality. So far the mass of the exponents of Irish nationality have contented themselves for over a century with words not deeds. When the moment came to fight there were either no fighters or no guns ... Unless the Irish in Ireland and most of all in America – where they are free and can act as they will – come forward now and give effective proof of their patriotism then they may bury the corpse of Irish nationality for ever, for no one will want to look at the stinking carcase any longer ... While we are saying that a German victory over England will bring

Ireland freedom, we, the most vitally concerned in that result, are not fighting for Ireland, or for Germany – but many thousands of Irishmen are fighting ... in the ranks of the British army ... The action so far taken by Irish Americans is contemptible - they have talked - floods of talk – but they have not even contributed money, much less attempted any overt act for Ireland ... If today, when all Europe is dying for national ends, whole peoples marching down with songs of joy to the valley of eternal night, we alone stand by idle or moved only to words, then are we in truth the most contemptible of all the peoples of Europe.

from a letter of Roger Casement to Joe McGarrity (April 1915)

**F  The Easter Rising was a military disaster and initially earned only the contempt of the Irish population. However the sacrifice of the rebels and their punitive treatment by the British soon turned them into the stuff of heroic myth. The ambiguity of the Irish response to the Rising was expressed by the poet, W.B.Yeats, a major figure in the Gaelic revival. He spoke of a 'terrible beauty', a reference to the terrible nature of violence and the uplifting beauty of sacrifice.**

> Too long a sacrifice
> Can make a stone of the heart.
> O when may it suffice?
> That is heaven's part, our part
> To murmur name upon name
> As a mother names her child
> When sleep at last has come
> On limbs that run wild.
> What is it but nightfall?
> No, no, not night but death;
> Was it needless death after all?
> For England may keep faith
> For all that is done and said.
> We know their dream, enough
> To know they dreamed and are dead;
> And what if excess of love
> Bewildered them till they died?
> I write it out in a verse-
> MacDonagh and MacBride
> And Connolly and Pearse
> Now and in time to be,
> Wherever green is worn,
> Are changed, changed utterly:
> A terrible beauty is born.

*Easter 1916* by W.B.Yeats, written in 1916, published in 1920

**G In the context of the contemporary carnage of the Western Front, the execution of only 16 of the 90 rebels who were condemned to death, does not now seem notably harsh. But that was not how it was perceived in Ireland at the time**

You remember the Jameson raid [in the Transvaal in 1895], when a number of [British] buccaneers invaded a friendly state, and fought the forces of the lawful government? If ever men deserved the supreme punishment it was they, but officially and unofficially, the influence of the British government was used to save them and it succeeded. You took care that no pleas of mercy should interpose on behalf of the poor young fellows who surrendered to you in Dublin. The first information which we got of their fate was the announcement that they had been shot in cold blood. Personally, I regard your action with horror, and I believe it has outraged the conscience of the country. Then the deporting of hundreds and even thousands of poor fellows without a trial of any kind seems to me an abuse of power as fatuous as it is arbitrary, and altogether your regime has been one of the worst and blackest chapters in the history of the misgovernment of the country.

from Bishop Edward O'Dwyer to General Maxwell, the British commander in Ireland (1916)

**H A journal, written by a Dublin woman during and after the Easter Rising, indicates how Irish attitudes softened towards the rebels and hardened towards Britain**

Of course this is not Ireland's rebellion - only a Sinn Fein rising ... How often have I laughed and quarrelled over the bare idea of an Irish Republic! It is so utterly un-Irish. Of course we want our own country free from foreign rule. But any one with sense must see that It must come by England's consent, not against England's will ...

The Sinn Fein leaders were such good men. They died like saints. Oh! the pity of it! and Ireland wanted them so much! They were men of such beautiful character – such high literary power and attainments – mystics, who kept the light burning. What madness came over them! And they were so splendid for the language. They lived such pure lives – as the priests who shrived them before execution said `The clean pure lives – the absolute resignation – may they pray for us, not we for them'. They have brought great and terrible trouble on us and Ireland – *but they meant to do the exact opposite.* They have crushed us under a weight of sorrow and shame – *but they meant the reverse.* What wild madness came over them!

But, as sure as God's sun rises in the East, if England doesn't get things right - if there's not immediately conciliation, and love and mercy poured out on Ireland - all the Sinn Fein leaders will be canonised! For their own merits. You know how Ireland is always merciful to the dead!

from *Landlord or Tenant?* by Magnus Magnussun (1978)

**I   In the wake of the Easter rising, Sinn Fein became increasingly influential. Having won 73 seats in the 1918 general election, it boycotted Westminster and established its own Irish parliament in Dublin with Eamonn de Valera, a survivor of the 1916 Rising, as its first President**
The Irish people is by right a free people. And whereas English rule in this country is and always has been based upon force and fraud and maintained by military occupation against the declared will of the people; and whereas the Irish Republic  was proclaimed in Dublin on Easter Monday, 1916, by the Irish Republican  Army acting on behalf of the Irish people; and whereas the Irish electorate has, in the general election of December 1918 declared by an overwhelming majority its firm allegiance to the Irish Republic.

Now therefore, we ratify the establishment of the Irish Republic and pledge ourselves and our people to make this declaration effective by every means at our command.

from the declaration of the *Dail Eireann* (January 1919)

**J   In the same year as the creation of the Dublin Parliament, the Irish Volunteers were reformed as the Irish Republican Army (IRA), which undertook guerilla warfare against the British forces and the terrorising of Irish civilians suspected of collaborating**
Travelling to his office just after after 9 am on a Dublin tram, reading his newspaper, Bell suddenly found two young men standing beside him as the tram stopped at a routine halt. 'Come on, Mr.Bell', said one of them. `Your time has come'. He was so aghast that he appeared to be unable to do or say anything. There was a moment of terrible suspense and anxiety in the crowded tram as everyone looked at each other in bewilderment. Nobody said a word. Then one of the young men spoke again: 'Ah, come on', he said, and he and his companion with the aid of some other young men who came down from upstairs forced Bell out of the tram and along the pavement to where, while he stood erect and apparently unperturbed, they shot him dead. His killers were undisguised and were described as 'respectable young men', who walked calmly away in a group and dispersed after 100 yards or so. Of the two passengers who came forward to try to do something for Bell, one had the use of only one arm. They called out, 'Is there nobody then to help us?'. But nobody dare come forward.

from *The Green Flag* by Robert Kee, quoting the inquest details as reported in the *Irish Times* (20 March 1920)

**K  The response of the British government was to employ still more coercion. A special irregular force, which included volunteers from among the less savoury inmates of British civilian and military gaols, was recruited to fight the IRA. Their hastily-designed khaki and black uniform earned them the nickname 'Black and Tans'. A British spokesman defined their role as a peace-keeping one**
They did not wait for the usual uniform, these Black and Tans who have joined the R[oyal] [Irish] C[onstabulary]. They came at once. They know what danger is. They have looked death in the eyes before and did not flinch. They will not flinch now. They will go on with the job - the job of making Ireland once again safe for the law-abiding, and an appropriate hell for those whose trade is agitation, and whose method is murder.

from a British government spokesman (1920)

**L  However, the terror and reprisals in which the Black and Tans engaged, while keeping the peace, led to their becoming the hated symbols of British authority in Ireland**
We find that the late Alderman MacCurtain, Lord Mayor of Cork, died from shock and haemorrhage caused by bullet wounds, and that he was wilfully murdered under circumstances of the most callous brutality, and that the murder was organised and carried out by the Royal Irish Constabulary, officially directed by the British government, and we return a verdict of wilful murder against David Lloyd George, Prime Minister of England; Lord French, Lord Lieutenant of Ireland; Ian MacPherson, late Chief Secretary of Ireland; Acting Inspector General Smith, of the Royal Irish Constabulary

from the jury verdict at a Cork inquest (March 1920)

Although Lloyd George claimed 'to have murder by the throat', the ferocity of 'the troubles' between 1919 and 1921 finally convinced him that a constitutional settlement acceptable to both Nationalists and Unionists had somehow to be found. A Government of Ireland Act (1920) had already created separate parliaments for Southern and Northern Ireland. Neither parliament had recognised the other, but their existence established a precedent and a basis for subsequent negotiation. In December 1921, after a tortuous series of discussions, the parties finally signed the Irish Treaty, according Southern Ireland Dominion status as the Irish Free State, with Ulster remaining part of the United Kingdom. This solved the major problem that had afflicted Anglo-Irish relations since the Union of 1800, but it left the Irish Nationalists deeply divided over the acceptability of the Treaty, which required the acceptance of partition and continued loyalty to the British Crown.

**M The disputed terms of the Anglo-Irish Treaty**
1 Ireland shall have the same constitutional status in the Community
of Nations known as the British Empire as the Dominion of Canada,
the Commonwealth of Australia, the Dominion of New Zealand, and
the Union of South Africa, with a Parliament having powers to make
laws for the peace, order and good government of Ireland and an
Executive responsible to that Parliament, and shall be styled and
known as the Irish Free State.
4 The oath to be taken by Members of the Parliament of the Irish Free
State shall be in the following form: I ... do solemnly swear true faith
and allegiance to the Constitution of the Irish Free State as by law
established and that I will be faithful to H.M. King George V, his heirs
and successors by law in virtue of the common citizenship of Ireland
with Great Britain and her adherence to and membership of the group
of nations forming the British Commonwealth of Nations ...

**N De Valera, leader of Sinn Fein and a survivor of the 1916 Rising,
explains why dominion status under the Crown is unacceptable**
The only banner under which our freedom can be won at the present
time is the Republican banner. It is as an Irish Republic that we have
a chance of getting international recognition ... Some might have
faults to find with that and prefer other forms of government. But we
are all united on this – that we want complete and absolute
independence ... This is the time to get freedom. Then we can settle
by the most democratic means what particular form of government
we may have.

**O A Nationalist rejects the Treaty on the grounds that by formalising
partition it denies Ireland real sovereignty**
I am opposed to the Treaty because it gives away our allegiance and
perpetuates partition. By that very fact that it perpetuates our slavery;
by the fact that it perpetuates partition it must fail utterly to do what it
is ostensibly intended to do – reconcile the aspirations of the Irish
people to association with the British Empire. When did the
achievement of our nation's unification cease to be one of our
national aspirations?
    ... the provisions of this Treaty mean this: that in the North of
Ireland certain people differing from us somewhat in tradition, and
differing in religion, which are very vital elements in nationality, are
going to be driven, in order to maintain their separate identity, to
demarcate themselves from us, while we, in order to preserve
ourselves against the encroachment of English culture, are going to
be driven to demarcate ourselves so far as ever we can from them. I
heard something about the control of education. Will any of the

Deputies who stand for it tell me what control they are going to exercise over the education of the Republican minority in the North of Ireland? They will be driven to make English, as it is, the sole vehicle of common speech and communication in their territory, while we will be striving to make Gaelic the sole vehicle of common speech in our territory. And yet you tell me that, considering these factors, this is not a partition provision. Ah! Sir, it was a very subtle and ironic master-stroke of English policy to so fashion these instruments that, by trying to save ourselves under them we should encompass our own destruction ...

from a speech by Sean MacEntee in the *Dail Eireann* (December 1921)

**P  In contrast the Unionists were now prepared to accept partition because they believed that a) having their own parliament in Northern Ireland would prevent them being dominated by the South, and b) the party-political situation in England left them no other choice**
We believe that so long as we were without a Parliament of our own, constant attacks would be made upon us, and constant attempts would be made to draw us into a Dublin Parliament, and that is the last thing in the world that we desire to happen. We profoundly distrust the Labour Party and we profoundly distrust the Rt. Hon. Gentleman the Member for Paisley (Mr Asquith). We believe that if either of those parties, or the two in combination, were once more in power our chances of remaining a part of the United Kingdom would be very small indeed. We see our safety, therefore, in having a parliament of our own, for we believe that once a parliament is set up and working well, as I have no doubt it would in Ulster, we should fear no one.

from a speech by Captain C.C.Craig in the Commons (March 1920)

**Q  In the bitter conflict that followed in Ireland after the Free State came into being in 1922, Michael Collins was the leader of the pro-Treaty forces while De Valera led those of the anti-Treaty. Collins, the Sinn Fein spokesman and one of the Irish signatories of the 1921 Treaty, explains why he is prepared to accept partition**
We have stated we would not coerce the northeast ... Surely we recognise that the northeast corner does exist, and surely our intention was that we should take such steps as would sooner or later lead to mutual understanding. The Treaty has made an effort, in my opinion, to deal with it on lines that will lead very rapidly to goodwill and the entry of the northeast under the British Parliament [applause]. I don't say it is an ideal arrangement, but if our policy is, as has been

stated, a policy of non-coercion, then let somebody else get a better way out of it.

from Collins's speech in the *Dail Eireann* (December 1921)

**R The failure of the Free State to meet Irish expectations is described by a veteran Nationalist politician**
My God, I thought that I would never live to see what is happening today under an Irish government. When we look back on the days when we were oppressed by England it would look like paradise if we could get the same sort of oppression now.

from John Dillon (January 1925)

# Q *uestions*

**1** Using sources A-C and your own knowledge, explain why the issue of support for Britain in the European war in 1914 caused deep divisions among Irish nationalists. **[7 marks]**

**2** How far does the evidence in sources D-F substantiate the claim that the Easter Rising of 1916 was a wholly unrealistic enterprise? **[8 marks]**

**3** Using sources G-I explain why the prevailing Irish attitude towards the 1916 rebellion changed from one of derision to one of admiration. **[7 marks]**

**4** In the light of sources J-L, comment on Lloyd George's claim in 1920 that the British authorities had 'murder by the throat'. **[9 marks]**

**5** In what ways do sources M-R illustrate both the strengths and limitations of the Anglo-Irish Treaty of 1921? **[9 marks]**

# 10 ANGLO-IRISH RELATIONS IN PERSPECTIVE

Although, as might be expected, Irish historical writing has tended to reflect the passion and intensity of the story being described, the marked feature of modern scholarship is the wide degree of convergence among historians. It is true that political activists still turn to Irish history in order to perpetuate their sense of grievance, but as the majority of the following sources show, reputable historians and commentators have long ago abandoned the pursuit of history as propaganda. English historians and those on both sides of the Irish border are intent on going behind the myths, powerful and many though these still are, to seek and reveal the truth.

**A  The popular broadcaster and writer, Magnus Magnusson, provides an effective summary of the way modern scholarship has helped to correct some of the false notions relating to modern Anglo-Irish history**

*Irish History–Fact or Fiction?* That is the challenging title of a recent booklet published in Ireland by the Churches Central Committee for Community Work. It was the outcome of a study of the influence of historical myths on Irish society and their emotive effect in the present situation, and it was aired at a conference entitled 'The Teaching of History – a Basis of Understanding, or a Cause of Disruption?' This conference, I may say, was attended by representatives from both the North and the South ... The mere fact that such an ecumenical conference should have been held at all in Ireland is a striking manifestation of the effect of the historiographical revolution. Fifty years ago, few people would even have dreamed of asking the question, never mind trying to find an answer to it.

However, in the 1930s, things began to change. In 1936, two young scholars founded societies to promote the scientific study of Irish history. In Belfast, Dr T.W. Moody, later a professor at Trinity College, Dublin, formed the Ulster Society for Irish Historical Studies; and in Dublin, Dr R.Dudley Edwards, now a professor at University College, Dublin, formed the Irish Historical Society. Then, in March 1938, the two societies, led by these revolutionary young historians, started publishing a joint journal, *Irish Historical Studies,* which has been published twice a year ever since.

Before then, Irish history had usually been a form of propaganda, not to be studied but to be quarried for material with which to support entrenched and dogmatic attitudes. Now the purpose was quite simply to try to encourage proper professionalism in the study of Irish history; to try to create standards of objective research and interpretation in an area previously riddled with prejudice and sectarianism and ignorance, both in the North and the South: in a word, to try to demythologise Irish history.

It is a very slow process. It has taken a long time for the new attitudes to percolate from the universities to the outside world, where Irish history is anything but an academic subject, but it is happening. A people who, because of the peculiar pressures that their past has placed on them might prefer to hold their historical myths inviolate, are actually beginning to ask questions like: 'Irish history – fact or fiction? ...

How these tensions thaw out eventually will ... depend to an extent on the way in which the Irish – and the British – learn to look at Irish history. Politicians, for instance, all tend to use history for their own ends, to justify what they are doing in the present or what they would like to see done. For instance, Sinn Fein used the Easter Rising most astutely to hallow their separatist policies – despite the fact that the overwhelming majority of Irishmen at the time did not care about separation from Britain ... At the same time, as Dr Conor Cruise O'Brien has argued (perhaps to his political cost), by making the Easter Proclamation the gospel of the Republic, Patrick Pearse's quasimystical concept of the need for violence and blood-sacrifice in every generation has become a justification not just for armed rebellions in the past but for violence and guerrilla warfare in the North today. In Ireland, as someone has said, history is a pack of tricks which the dead play on the living. Ireland is made of epigrams as well as epitaphs.

In the historiographical revolution, Irish historians are slowly defusing Irish history on both sides of the border as sacred writ to be cited as a categorical imperative to act in a certain way. We can only hope that eventually we will all learn to place the right emphasis on history as history, on mythology as mythology – and on today as today.

from *Landlord or Tenant: a View of Irish History* by Magnus Magnusson (1978)

**B Over 100 years ago, at a critical time in Irish affairs, the writer, A.G.Richey, argued that a knowledge of true history had a healing not a disruptive effect**

The study of Irish history does not excite political animosity but leads to the very opposite result. Thoroughly to appreciate the history of this or any country it is necessary to sympathise with all parties.

from *A Short History of the Irish People* by A.G.Richey (1869)

**C  The outstanding example of a revisionist writer concerned to challenge old assumptions and prejudices and to present Anglo-Irish relations in a balanced way is R.F.Foster**
The idea that Ireland underwent a process of 'modernisation' (economic, political and social) in the 19th century is much contested; certainly, a good deal of what characterized the country in the mid-20th century was obdurately pre-modern. Politics remained localist, parochial, clientelist; though it has been suggested that nationalism was a response to the process of modernisation, that theory begs the question of how far 20th-century politics were rooted in early 19th-century developments. The Irish case notoriously evades parallels with superficially 'similar' regions, Celtic or Continental. What is striking is how the different layers of the palimpsest of historical experience, laid down over many years, remained distinct in the Irish mind and led to a belief in deliverance. 'Our version of history', remarked the Bishop of Clonfert in 1957, 'has tended to make us think of freedom as an end in itself and of independent government - like marriage in a fairy story - as the solution to all ills'.

from *Modern Ireland 1600-1972* by R.F.Foster (1988)

**D  The same writer emphasises the importance of understanding the true character of the land issue as a factor in Irish politics**
What historians have to decide ... is the extent to which such [popular protest movements] are defined in terms of nationalist struggle; and to what extent they simply reflect local resentments on the perennial question of the land. 'Damn Home Rule!', George Birmingham was told by a local nationalist before independence, 'What we're out for is the land. The land matters. All the rest is tall talk'. Though this may have been what Birmingham (a Church of Ireland canon as well as a novelist) wanted to hear, it is a refrain repeated throughout Irish history. Travelling round Ireland before the Famine, Mr and Mrs S.C. Hall decided the same analysis was true of Ribbonism; General Lord Strathnairn concurred ('the possession of Irish land, on a sort of social principle, by the lower classes, is the aim of all Irish confederacies'). A hundred years later similar accusations were levelled in *Dail Eireann* at the motivation of some freedom fighters in the Anglo-Irish war ...

Researches into the 19th-century Irish economy at large, and the administration of Irish estates in particular, have produced a picture in which the flowing tide of prosperity is with its larger tenants; while the landlords, so far from raising rents to blood-sucking excesses, were charging at such an uneconomic level that they were bound for the dust-heap of history long before the combined efforts of Parnell, Davitt, Captain Moonlight and W.E.Gladstone finally precipitated them there. In fact the chief authorities on the late 19th-century Irish agrarian economy are positively critical of the Land Acts which pushed the landlords over the edge: one example of the way in which recent Irish scholarship carefully distinguishes economic history from the history of economic policy.

from the Introduction by R.F.Foster in *Nationalism and Popular Protest in Ireland,* ed. by C.H.E.Philpin (1987)

**E  Foster is also anxious to dispel the myths attaching to the record of Irish emigration**
The generalisations about Irish emigration remain based on the notion that it was invariably both proletarian and involuntary; and that it was inseparable from a sense of exile. This is taken to mean banishment from a territory – mental and spiritual as well as physical – which still imposes the psychological norms of reality, and exerts a compulsion to return which will never be fulfilled ... the fact that this does not seem to have been their invariable experience makes its imagery no less potent. It is certainly an inseparable component of expatriate Irish rhetoric; alienation persisted as a literary trope, even among the prosperous emigrants who had no intention of ever returning home. It was sustained by a long native tradition: religious poetry derived from the cult of St Columkille, the folk memory of Cromwellian transplantations, the romance of the Wild Geese. All these associations stressed the inseparability of Irishness and exile, and the links between Anglicisation and displacement. And this could be ingeniously utilised, as in a baroque petition to the Colonial Office on behalf of the Irish emigrants. 'Our feet, wearied night and day by exorbitant labour for impoverished masters, now tremble with feebleness whilst treading the paths of uncompensated toil. Our heads, long bent beneath a Slavish yoke, require support and encouragement towards their being raised to a natural consistency.'

from *Paddy & Mr Punch: Connections in Irish and English History* by R.F.Foster (1993)

**F  The orthodox Marxist view of Anglo-Irish history as the story of imperialism and class struggle is well illustrated by the following passage from an English writer**
The conquest of Ireland was the first step taken by England towards empire; and the methods the English rulers learned in Ireland provided the blueprints for their every subsequent act of conquest or suppression. Ireland was, indeed, the testing ground for all the policies of British imperialism. At the same time, there has been fought in Ireland the longest and most persevering of all struggles for

national liberation.

The relations between the English rulers and the Irish ruled have been, throughout, imperialist relations, consequently, the history of the 800 years of Anglo-Irish conflict – with its examples of every variety of imperialist aggression and of every form of resistance thereto – supplies an invaluable introduction to the critical study of imperialism in general ...

Irish writers upon the subject have commonly been satisfied with destroying such shreds of credit the English expounders of the quarrel have contrived to save. Thus they have, usually, missed the real tragedy involved in Ireland's history – the manner in which the English and Irish common people, each of them struggling for freedom, have been time and again jockeyed into becoming weapons used by the exploiters, each for the enslavement of the other ...

The English and the Irish common people, each with its own splendid record of unyielding resistance to oppression, should, by rights, understand each other better than they do, and be more ready than they have been to act in concert. Both together should find reasons for solidarity with the democratic and working-class struggles in other lands ...

I write frankly as a partisan. I have done my best to be candid; but impartiality is beyond my scope. My concern is to help forward the cause I uphold. If this book does that, even by a little, I shall have attained my object.

from *Ireland Her Own: an Outline History of the Irish Struggle* by T.A.Jackson (1971)

**G Conor Cruise O'Brien, a distinguished Irish scholar and statesman, indicates the difficulties that face contemporary historians attempting to write with detachment in an atmosphere of deep sectarian and political division**
Most history is tribal history: written that is to say in terms generated by, and acceptable to, a given tribe or nation, or a group within such a tribe or nation. If you know the language, etc, in which any 'standard' history of the origins of the First World War is written you will be able to make predictions, with a small margin of error, about its selection of data, conclusions on controversial points, and general emphasis. It would not be true to say that if you know the religion of an Irish historian you could make similarly accurate predictions. But it would not be true, either, to say that the choice of history textbooks in use in the Republic and in Northern Ireland, and in schools of the different denominations within each entity, has been unaffected by the sectarian context. Nor would it be true to say that the composition and production of schools of history in the various universities of

Ireland are altogether unaffected by the sectarian context within which these schools have historically developed, and in which they now exist. Historians, like other people, tend to identify with a community – not necessarily the one into which they were born – and in the case of modern historians this identification is likely to affect, and interact with, the character of their work, their career, their geographical location, and their public. Normally they write within a convention which suggests that these conditioning factors do not exist, or can be ignored. Marxist historians, indeed, emphasize such factors, but only as limitations on bourgeois historians.

To define [the Irish Question] as a national quarrel has arguments in its favour, but will not quite serve. What would the 'two nations' be? Irish Catholics do not, formally and consciously at least, think in terms of an Irish Catholic nation, but of an Irish nation including both Catholics and Protestants. Ulster Protestants do not – usually – regard themselves as not being Irish, but as Ulster folk, Irish but British as well, as the Scots and the Welsh are British. They regard Irish Catholics as fellow-Irishmen, but without this relationship in itself implying any cordiality: the Catholics are seen as disloyal fellow-Irishmen who refuse the common British bond uniting the rest of the people of the two islands, and who wish to impose a foreign status on people who intend to remain loyal. Nor is it tenable to assert, as most Provisionals seem to do, that it is a national quarrel between Ireland and England, with the mass of Protestants in the role of 'England's garrison'. Ulster Protestants form a community with a will of its own. The idea that contemporary England is manipulating the Protestants in order to 'keep its grip on Ireland' is part of the sick world of fantasy in which Sinn Fein lives.

from *States of Ireland* by Conor Cruise O'Brien (1972)

**H Nicholas Mansergh, a distinguished Irish analyst, suggests that too great a sense of detachment can lead historians to a loss of realism**
By virtue ... of their professional pre-occupation with enquiry and explanation, historians are apt to reduce to terms of cause and consequence matters about which contemporaries felt in terms of challenging, uplifting, desolating or terrifying personal experience. Destruction, violence, fear, intimidation, while given full play in polemical writings, are apt to figure in sophisticated historical works in the context of general analysis little calculated to pierce the consciousness of their readers. To the generation which experiences it, the effects of force upon their lives are real and tangible and the consequences of its use usually unpredictable; to succeeding generations the reverse obtains, the impact upon life becoming unreal, the outcome susceptible of statement with the result that

succeeding generations are disposed to exaggerate the consequences and to discount the price – especially in anniversary season. This is so even in an Irish setting, where war and civil war were episodic in character.

from *The Irish Question 1844-1921* by Nicholas Mansergh (1975)


**I   In his massive study of modern Irish history, Robert Kee points out the wide gap between nationalist aspirations and their achievement** Few Irishmen today would accept that what Irish nationalists have achieved represents a true fulfilment of that near-mystical ideal for which, in one form or another, Irishmen had striven for so long. Every mystical ideal is diminished by being translated into reality but the sense of diminishment in Ireland has been profound. One reason, in addition to the missing counties, is perhaps that the real substance of the aspirations that had made Irish history so tumultuous for a century and a half had already been achieved before the climax of these last years was reached.

What had kept the green flag flying throughout the period which Patrick Pearse saw as 'a hopeless attempt by a mob to realise itself as a nation' had been no doctrinaire concept of nationality but a much more simple human desire for a decent life, for an assurance of life at all, in the beautiful country in which Irishmen were born. The goal of 'freedom' was as vague as that and embraced a wide and diffuse political emotion. With the social revolution begun by the Land Acts and ending in the massive transfer of land-ownership through the long Land Purchase operation the greater part of this goal was quietly achieved. There remained only what might be called a debt to history, to be paid in the form of an award of that political self-respect which went with some form of Home Rule. For long years Irishmen had not been particularly insistent about this. And yet refusal to pay it, and a contemptuous refusal at that, stirred old memories and eventually led to an extraction of the debt after much bitterness and bloodshed in a compromise form of payment. In the course of this bitterness and bloodshed all the old emotions had been re-aroused.

James Connolly and other socialists had hoped to give the new nationalism a dynamic of its own, but socialism made little appeal to a nation of Catholic peasant proprietors with the traditions of an ancient Gaelic aristocracy deep in its folk memory. Even the cause of a united Ireland slumbered for nearly half a century before other, social grievances among the Catholic minority in Northern Ireland raised it again to embarrass not only the British government, but this time the Republic too.

from *The Green Flag* by Robert Kee (1972)

**J  F.S.L. Lyons, a major authority on Ireland, offers a definition of the Irish question**
The tired old witticism that every time the English came within sight of solving the Irish question the Irish changed the question, contains, like most jokes about Ireland, a small grain of truth submerged in a vast sea of misconception. The Irish did not change the question between the Famine and the war of independence any more than they had changed it between the Union and the Famine. The 'national demand', as it used to be called, remained in essence what Wolfe Tone had declared it to be as long ago as 1791, 'to break the connection with England, the never-failing source of all our political evils'. It is true, of course, that men differed in the 19th century, as they have continued to differ in the twentieth, about how complete the break should be, or more precisely, perhaps, about how far the full separatist ideal was practicable. But whether they took their stand on the rock of the republic, or were prepared to settle for repeal of the Union and some form of Home Rule based upon a reanimated Irish parliament, they were emphatic that the first step towards real independence was to recover for Irishmen the right to control their own affairs.

from *Ireland Since the Famine* by F.S.L.Lyons (1971)

**K  The same writer describes the changing emphases in modern interpretations of Irish history**
No ancient Israelite condemned to make bricks without straw can have been more embarrassed than the modern Irish historian who, in an unwary moment, agrees to write a general history of his country, even for so short and well-documented a period as the last 120 years. For although a work of synthesis is long overdue, it is not until one settles in earnest to the job of trying to provide it that one realises how much specialist study still needs to be undertaken. That there has been an historiographical revolution in the last 40 years nobody would deny, least of all myself, who has benefited from it more than most. Yet, by a paradox which is more apparent than real, although this revolution has to a large extent taken politics out of history, it has only been able to do so by concerning itself mainly with political history. Much of the most important research done on the 19th century during the past generation has revolved round the making and the breaking of the Union with Britain. Obviously this is a major theme, but the fact that students have allowed themselves to become obsessed with it has meant that other themes - economic, social, administrative, constitutional, cultural - have been seriously neglected.
    In the fields of economic and social history there have, indeed,

always been a few distinguished exceptions to this generalisation - and it is pleasant to record that their number is growing - but so many gaps in our knowledge remain to be filled that the general historian has either to admit ignorance and pass by on the other side, or else do some of the spade-work himself. I have adopted both procedures in this book, but where monographic studies have been conspicuously lacking, I have tried to supply at least a little of what we miss through their absence by providing rather more detail than is usually to be found in books of this kind.

from *Ireland Since the Famine* by F.S.L.Lyons (1971)

**L  An interesting perspective on Irish history is offered by D.G.Boyce, who suggests that the Anglo-Irish connection, far from being a handicap to Ireland was the necessary means by which the Irish developed a consciousness of their own political identity**
Ireland after the 17th century was not a colony, but a sister-kingdom and then, after 1800, an integral part of the British polity, inextricably linked with British politics, and, as always, exposed to British cultural influence. This made Irish political, social and economic development a concern of England in the way that the affairs of a remote dependency were not. England insisted on regulating the course of nationalism in Ireland from the late 18th century onwards; and this process of regulation enabled nationalism to develop and mature in a parliamentary and constitutional manner, although in the end it played into the hands of the physical force movement. It also enabled and encouraged a silent transfer of power to take place over most of Ireland, while in the end giving statutory recognition to the emergence of a particularist movement in north-east Ulster.

The English presence in and near Ireland did not make Irish nationalism 'worse' or 'better'; but, in a real sense, it made it possible. Ireland's political tradition, unlike that of, for example, France, had no independent existence, no clear-cut line of development. English constitutional reforms and the English language enabled nationalist Ireland to realise itself as a cultural and political entity over most of the country, fending off or containing the challenge of, on the cultural front, Irish Irelanders and Anglo-Irish literary patriots, and, on the political front, Irish Unionists and the revolutionary minority. Irish nationalism, therefore, was not peculiarly 'Irish'; on the contrary, its many paradoxes and self-contradictions arise from the close and permanent relationship between Ireland and her neighbour. And Ireland's dominant political tradition, like most aspects of her life, bears the ineradicable influence of England.

from *Nationalism in Ireland* by D.G.Boyce (1982)

**M Paul Johnson, journalist and historian, calls attention to the often overlooked degree of harmony that has existed in Anglo-Irish relations**

British-Irish relations are not so much a matter of human choice as of geographical determinism. 'God hath so placed us together unavoidably', to use a phrase of Milton's. If Irishmen who have resisted the British presence have sought aid from Britain's enemies - Spain and Rome, France and Germany, and today from those who finance and profit from international terrorism - so also Britain, in defending herself, has been obliged to bring Ireland into her calculations. There never will be a time when Britain will be able to remain indifferent to events in Ireland. To that extent, Britain will always have an 'Irish problem'; and, *a fortiori,* Ireland will always have an 'English problem'.

Yet we need not end on a note of despondency. Despite all the clashes between the English and the Irish, which necessarily form the substance of such a book as this, we must remember there is also a great unwritten and largely unrecorded story of Anglo-Irish relations: a story of countless friendships and innumerable intermarriages, of shared enthusiasms and dangers, mutual interests and common objectives. We have the same language and literature, the same legal tradition and parliamentary matrix. Whatever happens in the future, we can be sure that Irish and English will always have more to unite than to divide them.

from *Ireland: Land of Troubles* by Paul Johnson (1980)

# Q *u e s t i o n s*

**1** From a reading of source A what would you judge to be the major features of revisionism as applied to modern Irish history?

[8 marks]

**2** In sources C-E, what does R.F.Foster identify as the main questions calling for historical reassessment? [8 marks]

**3** In what ways does source F differ from sources B, G and H in its view of the need for objectivity in historical writing? [8 marks]

**4** How great a difference is there between sources I, J and K in their estimation of the importance of nationalism in modern Irish history?

[8 marks]

**5** How effective is the argument put forward in sources L and M that the Anglo-Irish connection has been not only beneficial, but essential to Ireland? [8 marks]

# 11 DEALING WITH EXAMINATION QUESTIONS

## Specimen Answers to Source-based Questions

*Questions based on Chapter 7 - 'Home Rule' (See pages 73-81).*

## Questions

1  In the light of sources A-E, describe the essential characteristics that Parnell brought to the the Home Rule movement. **(7 marks)**

2  In what respects do sources F and H differ from source G in their interpretation of Home Rule? **(7 marks)**

3  What insights are offered by sources I, K, L and P into the reasons for the split in the Liberal ranks over Home Rule? **(10 marks)**

4  Using your own knowledge and the evidence in sources M-O, explain the circumstance in which Parnell came to lose the leadership of the Irish Parliamentary Party in 1890. **(8 marks)**

5  Assess the value to the historian, studying Irish nationalism, of sources Q, R and S. **(8 marks)**

### Points to note about these questions

1  You are required here to draw your ideas exclusively from the sources.

2  Again, your analysis should relate only to the sources. Your own background knowledge is not requested.

3  Here your own knowledge is essential if you are to interpret the sources effectively.

4  You are required here, in effect, to write, a mini-essay describing the circumstances surrounding Parnell's fall, illustrating this with choice references to the designated sources.

5  This a very different type of evaluation from the preceding questions. Here you need to assess the strengths and weaknesses (if any) of the sources as historical documents, concentrating on their value as evidence of the character of Irish nationalism.

## SPECIMEN ANSWERS

1  In the light of sources A-E, describe the essential characteristics that
   Parnell brought to the the Home Rule movement.          **(7 marks)**

As shown in sources A and B, Isaac Butt was essentially moderate and
constitutional in his approach. His idea of Irish independence was a
limited federal one. He believed that Home Rule could be achieved by
persuading `liberal-minded' English MPs to accept the notion of a
restricted measure of self government for Ireland. Parnell rejected such
moderation; he shows in source C that he does not regard the English
Parliament as sufficiently sympathetic ever to grant Home Rule. Realism
demands that the Commons be forced into considering the issue. James
O'Kelly draws attention to Parnell's ability to strengthen the presentation
of the Irish case by uniting the conservative and radical nationalists.
O'Kelly further suggests that Parnell's powerful personality and
leadership skills will create a determined lobby in the Commons and
attract the support of Irish opinion at large. Justin McCarthy re-
emphasises these points and lays particular stress on the success of the
disruptive parliamentary tactics that Parnell employed in order to force
the Irish question on the attention of the Commons in the only way
possible.

2  In what respects do sources F and H differ from source G in their
   interpretation of Home Rule?                            **(7 marks)**

Gladstone argues in source F that the Irish must have a more direct say
in the running of their own affairs. He regards the solving of the land
question, involving the settling of the landlord-tenant dispute, as essential
to peace in Ireland. This can best be achieved, he believes, against a
background of genuine local self government for Ireland. In H,
Gladstone defines his concept of Home Rule: the Union would continue
to operate, there would be no need for a separate Irish parliament, the
Protestant minority would be safeguarded, and financial responsibilities
would be shared appropriately. The granting of such concessions,
Gladstone hopes, would prevent the Nationalists from playing the
English parties against each other.

   In contrast, Parnell (G) will accept no limitation on Irish independence. He urges as a first stage the restoration of a separate Irish
parliament. Parnell does not specify his exact demands, but with his
rhetorical appeal to the irresistible march of nations he strongly implies
that the ultimate goal is complete separation and independence for
Ireland.

3  What insights are offered by sources I, K, L and P into the reasons for
   the split in the Liberal ranks over Home Rule?          **(10 marks)**

Source I indicates that Gladstone was well aware that if he introduced an
Irish Home Rule Bill the Whig element in his Party would refuse to
support him. Hartington, the leader of the Whigs, was adamant in his
opposition to repeal of the Union. In this respect the Whigs were little
different from the Conservatives. The Liberal Party was an uneasy
coalition of Whigs, radicals and Gladstonites. If Hartington persisted in
opposing Home Rule, Gladstone's position as Party leader would become
impossible. On the radical left of the Party, Joseph Chamberlain was not
against a limited degree of local self government for Ireland but he
pledges (J) his total opposition to Home Rule as envisaged by Parnell.
Chamberlain's view is that such a measure, as Gladstone seems to be
contemplating, would not merely break the link between Britain and
Ireland; it would destroy the integrity of the British Empire.

   1886 was, therefore, a critical year in Liberal fortunes. Despite the
looming difficulties, Gladstone pressed ahead with his Home Rule Bill.
When he introduced it in the Commons (K) he presented it as a matter
of principle that went beyond party politics, an interpretation that
neither the Whigs nor the radicals could accept. Notwithstanding a
brilliant parliamentary performance on Gladstone's part, the Bill was
defeated on its second reading, over 90 Liberals voting with the
Conservatives against it. This marked a deep division in the Liberal Party,
many of whose members broke away with Chamberlain to join the
Conservative Party, who as `Unionists' had played the Orange card. In
the aftermath of the Liberals' defeat, the Unionists, with Balfour as
Irishman Secretary (L), and free of the incubus of Home Rule, followed
a dual policy of concession and firmness. Despite Liberal divisions,
Gladstone continued his campaign for Home Rule. His second Bill was
passed by the Commons but thrown out by a Unionist-dominated House
of Lords (P). It would be nearly another 30 years before the Liberal Party
would be in a position to re-introduce Irish Home Rule.

4  Using your own knowledge and the evidence in sources M-O, explain
   the circumstance in which Parnell came to lose the leadership of the
   Irish Parliamentary Party in 1890.          **(8 marks)**

Parnell's political star was very much in the ascendant in the late 1880s
following the revelation that *The Times's* attempt to portray him as a
supporter of the Phoenix Park murders of 1882 had been based on
forged documents (M). However, his personal life was to be his political
undoing. For some years Parnell had had a sexual liaison with Kitty
O'Shea, wife of Captain O'Shea, a nationalist MP. This was one of those
Victorian open secrets that did not become a scandal unless it was openly
admitted and became public knowledge. This duly happened in 1890;

Parnell was cited as co-respondent by O'Shea in a divorce action against his wife. Parnell made no attempt to defend himself. Gladstone feared that if he were to continue his political relationship with an admitted adulterer then the Nonconformists, a major support group of the Liberals, would abandon the Liberal Party. Consequently, he let it be known that he could no longer contemplate co-operating with Parnell (N).

This obliged the Irish MPs to reconsider their own position. As shown by the leader in the *Nation* (O), an influential voice of Irish nationalism, there were many among the Irish MPs at Westminster who felt they could not continue supporting Parnell. After an acrimonious meeting, a majority of these MPs voted against Parnell's remaining as leader. Following this, Catholic opinion in Ireland hardened against him. The Irish bishops and clergy who until then had maintained a discreet silence now felt obliged to urge their flock to disassociate themselves from a Protestant adulterer. For a time Parnell tried to carry on, but his cause was now a hopeless one.

5   Assess the value of sources Q, R and S to the historian, studying Irish
    nationalism.                                                      **(8 marks)**

With the defeat of Gladstone in 1886 and the return of the Conservatives to power, thoughts of Home Rule had to be temporarily suspended. One reaction was a re-emphasis in Ireland upon the traditional Gaelic national character. Archbishop Croke, a leading proponent of Irish national self-awareness, advocates (Q) a rejection of English manners and pastimes and a return to the traditional sports and ways of life of old Ireland. Douglas Hyde develops the same argument with reference to indigenous Irish arts and culture (R). Hyde adds significantly that a return to Irishness is not simply a `moral' question; it relates to Ireland's ability to develop a separate self-sustainable economy. Both Q and R provide the historian with striking examples of the cultural and intellectual arguments in support of a Gaelic revival.

James Connolly's viewpoint (S) is in sharp contrast to Q and R. As a Marxist, he contends that only through proletarian revolution, the rising of the Irish workers, will Ireland be able to throw off the yoke of British imperialism and fulfil its true destiny as a workers' republic. For Connolly, Gaelic history is of little value in itself if it is not used to stimulate revolution, the first step towards which must be the seizure by the working class of the key positions of power in Ireland. That is how to interpret `Sinn Fein', not in a nationalistic sense, but in a dialectical one. Interesting though Connolly's ideas are for the historian, it has to be said that they were very much minority ones. Despite his legendary role in the 1916 Easter Rising, Connolly was never more than a fringe influence in Irish national affairs.

# Preparing Essay Answers

Contrary to popular belief, examiners do not enjoy failing candidates. The problems are largely made in the examination room by the candidates themselves. As the reports of the examination boards point out year after year, the greatest single weakness among examinees is an inability to be relevant in their answers. No matter how well read and knowledgeable candidates may be, if they stray too far from the terms of the question they cannot be given credit. Examinations from A level upwards are basically a test of the candidates' ability to analyse historical material in such a manner as to present a reasoned, informed, response to a specific question. Too often examiners are faced with regurgitated notes on a set of topics, little of which relates to the questions as set. There really is no such animal as an `easy' exam question at these levels; those who set the papers seldom repeat the exact wording of their questions. This means that each question demands its own individual interpretation. The intelligence and subtlety of the candidates' response will determine how high a mark they score. Examinees must, of course, have `knowledge', but academic history tests not only *what* they know but how well they *use* what they know.

As an aid to the development of effective examination technique, here is a list of questions that candidates should ask themselves when preparing their essays:

1 *Have I answered the question AS SET* or have I simply imposed my prepared answer on it? (It is remarkable how many exam scripts contain answers to questions that do not appear on the exam paper!)

2 *Have I produced a genuine argument* or have I merely put down a number of disconnected points in the hope that the examiners can work it out for themselves? (Too many answers consist of a list of facts rounded off by the `Thus it can be seen ...' type of statement which seldom relates to what has been previously written.)

3 *Have I been relevant in arguing my case* or have I included ideas and facts that have no real relation to the question? (Some candidates simply write down all they know about a topic, assuming that sheer volume will overwhelm the examiner into giving a satisfactory mark. This `mud-at-the-wall' method is counter-productive since it glaringly exposes the candidate's inability to be selective or show judgement.

4 *Have I made appropriate use of primary or secondary sources to illustrate my answer?* (Examiners do look for evidence of intelligent reading. Choice, apt, quotation from documents or books does elevate the quality of an answer. Acquaintance with the ideas of modern historians and authorities is a hallmark of the better-prepared candidate.

However, discretion needs to be shown; putting in quotations where they are not relevant or inserting over-long, rote-learned passages merely looks like padding.)

5 *Have I tried to show originality* or have I just played safe and written a dull, uninspired answer? (Remember, examiners have to plough through vast quantities of dreary, ill-digested material from large numbers of candidates. When, therefore, they come across a script that shows initiative and zest, their interest and sympathy are engaged. A candidate who applies his or her own reasoning and interpretation to a question may occasionally make naive statements but, given that the basic understanding and knowledge are sound, the candidate's ambition will be rewarded. This is not an encouragement to `waffle', but it is to suggest that, provided always that he or she keeps to the terms of the question, the candidate is free to follow his or her own judgements. A thought-provoking answer is likely to be a good answer.)

# Possible Essay Titles

1 Why was the Act of Union passed in 1800?

This is a deceptively easy-looking question. One obvious part of the answer is that the British government and Parliament wanted union as a means of quietening the troubles in Ireland and guarding their flank against France. However, as much attention needs to be paid to the reasons for the Irish acceptance of the measure. Here mention should be made of the bribe of emancipation which aroused the political as well as the religious expectations of the Catholic Irish. It would also be relevant to analyse the attitudes of George III, Pitt and the cabinet towards the emancipation issue. It is important to emphasise that the Act of Union was very much the result of short-term thinking.

2 With what justification has Daniel O'Connell been described as 'the great liberator'?

Some account of the scale of O'Connell's activities is necessary, and this is best presented chronologically. His skills as a politician, his ability to organise the Catholic Irish into a force effective enough to win emancipation in 1829: these should be stressed. However, the answer will show balance if as much space is devoted to post-1830 developments as to pre-1830. O'Connell's battles over the 1832 Reform Bill, tithes and repeal of the Union need to be examined. The fact that he was superseded in regard to aims and methods by Young Ireland suggest that the latter part of his career was less successful. Nonetheless, his earlier achievements were real enough and he became the symbol of Irish resistance. He had politicised Irish Catholicism.

3 Consider the view that the granting of Catholic emancipation in 1829 changed the character of Irish politics.

Emancipation certainly altered the political balance in Ireland. It made the prospect of the repeal of the Union a terror to the Protestant north, for, if an Irish parliament were to be restored, Catholics would dominate it. Combative Protestantism began to organise itself. This prompted the more radical nationalist and Catholic movements to increase their agitation for repeal of the Union. The gaining of Relief in 1829 was interpreted by such groups as an example of the concessions that could be forced from the British if only enough pressure was brought to bear. It was no coincidence that O'Connell adopted direct parliamentary agitation after 1829 or that movements such as Young Ireland developed, committed to achieving political change, and not just religious or social reform.

4 Examine the legacy of the Great Famine of the 1840s.

There are two distinct aspects worth pursuing; the economic and the political. The scale of the famine devastated particular areas and stimulated population shift, emigration, and eventually better land use. However, it would show understanding of modern research to emphasise that the Famine did not so much create as accelerate already existing trends. On the political front, the famine produced a bitterness in the Irish which derived from their belief that the English government had declined to relieve the suffering. Such anger stimulated the growth of radical movements in Ireland, from Young Ireland to Fenianism. Widespread outrages occurred; the British authorities replied with a series of coercion acts between 1847 and 1857. The stage was set for decades of violent action and reaction.

5 Did C.S.Parnell do more to advance or to retard the cause of Irish independence?

The implication of the question is that Parnell's fall in 1890 and the split in the Nationalist ranks that followed, led to the weakening of the case for Home Rule and its shelving for over a generation, by which time the difficulties in its way were even greater than they had been in the 1880s. This is a sustainable case, but it overlooks the enormous contribution Parnell had made during his period of leadership. He was not always successful, as his chequered relations with Gladstone showed, but his powers of organisation and leadership at a critical juncture in Irish affairs have to be acknowledged. Apart perhaps from O'Connell, no Irishman, Catholic or Protestant, had been able to impose himself so effectively on English attention, and thereby force government and parliament to respond to Irish demands.

6  Who came closest to resolving the Irish question in the late 19th century, the Liberals or the Conservatives?

It is arguable that for all his good intentions Gladstone never truly grasped the political nature of the question. His various measures to do with land, religion, and education were intended to create an Irish `content' by solving each part of the problem piecemeal. Even when he came to accept that Home Rule was necessary, he still saw it as an ameliorative measure rather than the granting of full independence. The Conservatives were much clearer in perception and aim. They rejected Home Rule because it undermined the integrity of the United Kingdom and betrayed Ulster. They were, however, prepared to tackle the outstanding grievance – landlord-tenant relations. The Conservative reforms culminating in Wyndham's Act of 1903 may be said to have settled the land question in Ireland. By then, of course, Ulster had created an extra political dimension to the Irish question.

7 How realistic were the aims of the *Sinn Fein* movement before 1922?

It is important here to define the aims. These, of course, changed tactically according to circumstance. Sinn Fein was a product of the Gaelic revival but went way beyond it in political objective. It wanted a separate geographically-united Irish nation with its own parliament, totally free of British control. It could be said to be unrealistic in its over-estimation of the degree of support it had among the Irish nation, and its under-estimation of British resolve in a time of war, hence the collapse of the Easter Rising. It also failed to understand the moral case or strength of purpose of fellow Nationalists or Ulster loyalism. With these observations as reference points, an assessment of the degree of success achieved by the movement between 1906 and 1922 is required.

8 Did Asquith's Liberal government have a mandate for Home Rule?

The official Liberal Party had been committed to Home Rule since 1886, but it was the Parliament Act of 1911 that made it possible for the Liberals to re-introduce the measure in 1912. The Lords could no longer destroy the Bill as they had in 1894. However, this was not the same as possessing a mandate. The two elections of 1910 had wiped out the Liberals' majority and made them dependent on the Irish MPs. Unionists argued that so major a change as Home Rule flew in the face of constitutional precedent by subjecting the Ulster Protestants, a substantial majority in their own region, to the whim of a hung parliament. The Unionist case was that so identifiable a political and national entity as the Ulster loyalists had to be consulted before their fate was decided. Asquith's government in effect conceded this by suspending the implementation of the the Bill in 1914.

9 `An unrealistic venture, doomed from the start': comment on this view of the Easter Rising of 1916.

Although its timing seemed propitious, England being heavily committed on the Western Front, insufficient care had gone into the planning of the Rising. Liaison was confused, arms were lacking, and no clear plan of campaign had been established. The romanticism of Pearse and the socialist tenacity of Connolly could not make up for these deficiencies. Moreover, on the admission of the rebels themselves, the Rising could be successful only if the Irish people joined in nationwide. This they markedly failed to do. The swift and determined British response was in sharp contrast to the ineptitude of the planning. The derision and contempt with which Dubliners originally greeted the Rising illustrated how out of touch with reality its organisers had been. It was the courage of the defeated rebels allied to British severity that later turned farce into heroic myth.

10 How effectively did the Treaty of 1921 solve the Irish Question?

In one sense the answer is – very effectively – since it extricated Britain from a problem that had dogged her since the Union of 1800. However, it did so at the cost of lasting bitterness. Although the Unionists accepted the Treaty they did so only on the guarantee of partition, a form of settlement wholly rejected by a substantial segment of Irish nationalist opinion. The consequence was a savage civil war in Southern Ireland immediately after the Irish Free State came into being. The Treaty did not so much solve the Irish question as alter the terms in which the question was perceived. The difficulties experienced by the Irish Free State and the unresolved issue of the status of Ulster were proof that the Irish question had not gone away; it had simply changed its form.

# Specimen Essay Answer

### Why, despite Catholic Emancipation, was there still an `Irish Question' in 1868?

The most immediate response to this question is to suggest that the `Irish Question' was about much more then Catholic emancipation. It had a number of components. Over-population and land-hunger, grievances over religion, landlord-tenant relations, and education were among the key factors. However, over all there was a political issue – the repeal of the Union. As subsequent history before and beyond 1868 was to show, until the political issue was solved there could be no settlement of the Irish Question.

Disraeli defined the Irish question in these terms: `A dense and starving population inhabits an island where there is an Established Church which is not their Church. Over them rules a territorial aristocracy the richest of whom live in distant capitals. In addition they have the weakest executive in the world.'

Disraeli was referring to the fact that the established English Protestant Church was maintained by tithes levied on the people, yet represented barely 7 per cent of the Irish population. His comment on the land question referred to the situation in which the native Irish peasantry lived a precarious existence on land that they could not own because it was in the possession of absentee English landlords who could evict them at will. The `starving population' was the mass of the over-populated Irish peasants, hungry for land and food. The `weakest executive' was a reference to the English government's policy of controlling Ireland by means of a Protestant pro-English administration in Dublin.

Gladstone also provided a picture of the Irish Question. He likened the problems of Ireland to the legendary Upas tree whose poisoned branches were the land, education and the Church. Gladstone also declared that `the state of Ireland after 700 years of our tutelage is an intolerable disgrace', showing how deep-seated the problem was historically. One single amelioration, such as emancipation, could not solve this.

How basic the political issue is to an understanding of why the granting of emancipation did not solve the Irish question can be judged by surveying Anglo-Irish developments between 1829 and 1868. Having achieved emancipation, O'Connell went on in the 1830s to build an Irish party of MPs at Westminster which pressed for the disestablishment of the Anglican Church in Ireland. A number of Whig reforms in the 1830s weakened the Anglican grip upon the State apparatus. This encouraged O'Connell to begin a campaign for the repeal of the Act of Union. However, Catholic emancipation had transformed Irish politics. Protestant supremacy was now challenged and Protestants began to organise in defence of the Union. This frustrated O'Connell's efforts and Young Ireland, a group of younger activists, emerged. They rejected O'Connell's constitutional methods and advocated violence.

The 1840s, in Irish history, were dominated by the Great Famine, which overwhelmed an Irish population which had doubled since 1801. The bitterness of the experience was deepened by the perceived failure of the English government to take steps to end the misery. Young Ireland adopted a policy aimed at the forcible expulsion of the English. Planned outrages occurred widely, to which Parliament responded with twelve coercion acts between 1847 and 1857. These created further violence leading to the creation in 1857 of the Irish Republican Brotherhood. This Fenian movement claimed to be the true authority of Ireland, asserting that the country was independent but temporarily in bondage to England. The IRB instigated a series of bombings in mainland Britain during the 1860s.

It was in this atmosphere that Gladstone began his attempt in 1868 to tackle the underlying problems in Anglo-Irish relations. These, as the intervening years since emancipation had shown, were an amalgam, of religious, economic, educational and above all political grievances. Until these were resolved the `Irish Question' would remain.

# BIBLIOGRAPHY

It will come as no surprise to the student to learn that there is an ever-growing wealth of books on Ireland and Anglo-Irish relations. The following list is a very selective set of suggestions as to some of the most accessible and readable works:

**J.C.Beckett:** *The Anglo-Irish Tradition* (Faber & Faber 1976). An important set of essays on relations between Ireland and England.

**J.C.Beckett:** *The Making of Modern Ireland* (Faber & Faber 1972). The same author's much admired survey of Irish history.

**D.G. Boyce:** *Ireland 1828-1923* (Blackwell 1992). A brief but enlightening survey of the period.

**D.G.Boyce:** *Nationalism in Ireland* (Croom Helm 1982). A lively account of some of the cross-currents of Irish history.

**D.G.Boyce and Alan O'Day (eds):** *Parnell in Perspective* (Routledge 1991). A collection of essays introducing the latest research on a critical figure in a critical period of Irish history.

**D.G.Boyce (ed):** *The Revolution in Ireland 1879-1923* (Macmillan 1988). Another set of essays by experts on major themes.

**T. P.Coogan:** *De Valera, Long Fellow, Long Shadow* (Hutchinson 1993). The latest work by a lively and regular contributor to the debate on Irish history.

**T.P.Coogan:** *Ireland Since the Rising* (Pall Mall Press 1966). An important earlier study by the same writer.

**R.F.Foster:** *Modern Ireland 1600-1972* (Penguin 1988). Arguably the best book on Ireland currently available, scholarly, provocative and up-to-date.

**R.F.Foster:** *Paddy and Mr Punch: Connections in Irish and English History* (Allen Lane, The Penguin Press 1993). A more difficult book by the same author, but well worth reading for its analysis of Anglo-Irish attitudes.

**T.A.Jackson:** *Ireland Her Own: an Outline History of the Irish Struggle* (Lawrence and Wishart 1971). First written in 1938, this is well worth reading as an example of a committed Marxist-Nationalist interpretation of Irish history.

**Robert Kee:** *The Green Flag: a History of Irish Nationalism* (Weidenfeld and Nicolson 1972). A must - a large, well-illustrated and informative study.

**Robert Kee:** *The Laurel and the Ivy: the story of Charles Stewart Parnell and Irish Nationalism* (Hamish Hamilton 1993). Another monumental study, this time of Parnell, the outstanding figure in 19th-century Anglo-Irish relations.

**J.J.Lee:** *Ireland 1912-1985* (CUP 1989). An interesting Nationalist perspective on the later part of the period.

**F.S.L.Lyons:** *Ireland Since the Famine* (Weidenfeld and Nicolson 1971). Described by other scholars as a 'magisterial' study of Irish history.

**Magnus Magnusson:** *Landlord or Tenant: a View of Irish History* (The Bodley Head 1978). An excellent popular treatment of Anglo-Irish relations, full of stimulating observations.

**Nicholas Mansergh:** *The Irish Question 1844-1921* (George Allen & Unwin 1975). Now established as a major work by a major historian.

**T.W.Moody and F.X.Martin:** *The Course of Irish History* (Mercier Press 1967). An excellent introduction to Irish history, covering a wide field.

**Conor Cruise O'Brien:** *States of Ireland* (Hutchinson 1972). Contains some of this important writer's key ideas on Irish history.

**Alan O'Day and John Stevenson (eds):** *Irish Historical Documents since 1800* (Barnes & Noble 1992). A very useful source book with linking commentary.

**Patrick O'Farrell:** *Ireland's English Question* (Batsford 1971). As its title suggests, this reverses the customary way of looking at Anglo-Irish history.

# INDEX